18C

D0930105

# PEDAGOGY IN PROCESS

# PEDAGOGY IN PROCESS

The Letters to Guinea-Bissau

## PAULO FREIRE

TRANSLATED BY
CARMAN ST. JOHN HUNTER

A CONTINUUM BOOK
THE SEABURY PRESS · NEW YORK

1978 · The Seabury Press
815 Second Avenue · New York, N.Y. 10017

Original title: *Cartas à Guiné Bissau: Registros de uma experiencia em processo;*
translated by Carman St. John Hunter and edited by Martha Keehn
from the original Portuguese manuscript.

*Printed in the United States of America*

*Library of Congress Cataloging in Publication Data*
Freire, Paulo, 1921-     Pedagogy in process.
(A Continuum book)
Translation of Cartas à Guiné Bissau.
1. Reading (Adult education)—Guinea-Bissau.
2. Elementary education of adults—Guinea-Bissau.
3. Freire, Paulo, 1921-     I.Title.
LC5225.R4F7313     374.9'66'57     78–2678     ISBN 0–8164–9339–1

*Dedicated to the memory of
Amilcar Cabral,
educator, who learned from his people.*

---

*"I may have my opinion about many things,
about the way
to organize the struggle; the way to organize the
Party;
an opinion, for example, that I formed in
Europe, in Asia,
or in some other country of Africa, from
reading books
or documents, from meetings which influenced
me. I cannot,
however, pretend to organize a Party or a
struggle on
the basis of my own ideas. I have to do this
starting
from the reality of the country."*
—AMILCAR CABRAL

# CONTENTS

# FOREWORD

It will come as no surprise to North American readers—not those, at least, who have read the earlier work of Paulo Freire —to learn that he has not gone into exile in Geneva in order to escape from history.

On the contrary, as these letters and the introductory essay will quite eloquently attest, Freire is too much a man of praxis to rest very long upon nostalgia for the past, nor even upon the passionate recollection of that past.

It is Fidel Castro who said that the duty of a revolutionary is "to make the revolution." If Freire's efforts in Brazil and Chile have been arrested, in the short run, by the not-so-subtle operations of the C.I.A., or of those governments imposed upon the people of both nations by domestic rulers who conduct their business in collaboration with the North American and European corporations, Freire himself is unwilling to sit still within an office in Geneva, nor to "perform on orders" for a liberal audience in San Francisco or New Delhi. Instead, he is industriously at work in building that revolution, made of "words that shape the world," in several newborn African nations at this hour.

It would be tempting here to speak again about the basic themes—the "generative words" and "codifications"—of Freire's pedagogic work among (and with) the desperately poor peasants of Brazil. It would be interesting, also, to attempt to summarize those themes as they are stated once again within the essay that precedes the letters which comprise most of the present book. To do this, however, is to re-run once again the subject-matter of his previous work. It seems far more important, and more human in this case, to speak of these beautiful letters in themselves.

The book, for which these letters provide both core and rationale, will not only broaden the already substantial audience for Freire's work. It will also clarify his views, and humanize the man himself, for those who still regard him as an ominous or intimidating person, rather than as the very gentle and, at all times, open and affectionate human being that both his friends and pupils know so well.

Apart from all else, the book provides the best, most idiomatic English version of his writing to this date. More important, it reveals him—in the company of Elza—in a series of specific situations and direct, emotional relationships with other educators. Thus, not only the translation, but the letter-genre *in itself,* gives English-speaking readers, at long last, a direct sense of the character of Paulo Freire: a character full of warmth, of humble attitude and militant fervor, all in a single man and oftentimes expressed within a single word or phrase.

It is not surprising that the human side of Paulo Freire has, up to this time, gone largely unperceived. The format of his earlier writings, that of the didactic essay, denies the exposition of those very characteristics which most faithfully reflect the goals and nature of the man. The conversational tone made possible by an exchange of correspondence provides, for the first time, an appropriate literary metaphor for the man who has made "dialogue" almost a synonym for "education."

Freire gives this collection of letters an appropriate title: *Pedagogy in Process.* It is an ideal title for a book that records, by measured and unhurried stages, the evolution of a "pedagogic partnership" between Freire (and his colleagues at the World Council of Churches), on the one hand, and the educators of the new-born nation, Guinea-Bissau, on the other. Their common purpose is to develop a literacy program for a newly liberated people.

The correspondence begins as a one-to-one exchange between Freire, writing from Geneva, and Mario Cabral of Guinea-Bissau. Soon, however, the correspondence broadens out to include the other members of the "team"—members both in Africa and in Geneva. In spite of the foreshortened time-span of the letters (January, 1975 to spring of 1976), the repercussions of the dialogue—as noted in a recent and nostalgic postscript—extend into 1977 and beyond. They also extend beyond one nation's borders, leading to collective literacy efforts planned by several of the new nations of Africa—all sharing the heritage of many centuries of European domination.

Those who wonder what an exiled educator from Brazil, now resident in Switzerland, might have in common with the people of a land like Guinea-Bissau, will, no doubt, settle first upon the simple fact of a shared heritage of servitude, as stated just above. The deeper bond, however, lies in Freire's revolutionary posture, one that is shared by his co-workers and in this case, "correspondents," within Guinea-Bissau. The education of an oppressed and struggling people, as he insists at several points, must, from the first, be both political and non-neutral—or it never can succeed.

A corollary to this point, as stated and restated several times in Freire's work, is that any group of "outside educators" who have grown up, lived and studied, in a privileged situation, must "die as a class" and be reborn in consciousness—learning always even while they teach, and working always "with" (not "on") the nations and the people that invite their aid. ("Collaboration," as opposed to "cultural invasion," is the crucial term.)

In view of Freire's conviction of the need for a militant and revolutionary stance on both sides of the pedagogic coalition which he first proposes, then creates and finally records, readers may find it paradoxical that I have described him as an "affectionate" and "gentle" human being. It is Freire himself, however, who provides the answer to this seeming paradox.

In one of his frequent references to Che Guevara—a man he has described, in earlier work, as one of the great models of a self-effacing teacher—Freire draws upon one of the phrases first identified with Che: "Let me say, with the risk of appearing ridiculous, that the true revolutionary is guided by strong feelings of love."*

It is the triumph of this motivation, above all else, in the work and in the life of Paulo Freire, that render his unevasive revolutionary posture so disarming to those who otherwise would cringe at the first recognition of his true intent.

It is that same motivation—revolutionary passion, born of the most selfless love—that makes his newest book the one which is most certain to extend his vision and his consciousness of pedagogic struggle to those in every continent, in every land, who *need* that vision and that consciousness the most.

"I would like to engage in dialogue with you and your co-workers. . . ."

Freire has spoken words like these, no doubt at least a thousand times by now, in starting a workshop, seminar or simple conversation. In "The Letters to Guinea-Bissau," he broadens the dialogue at last, to reach more than a highly educated few. It is, therefore—while not his classic work—unquestionably his most accessible. By my own taste, it is also his most powerful —and human.

JONATHAN KOZOL

*Boston*
*January 1978*

---

*Venceremos—The Speeches and Writings of Che Guevera,* edited by John Gerassi (New York: Macmillan, 1969), p. 398.

# INTRODUCTION

## Part One

This introduction is, above all, a letter-report that I make to the reader. It will be as informal as the letters contained in the body of the book. I shall attempt, as though in conversation with the reader, to emphasize this or that significant aspect that has impressed me in my working visits to Guinea-Bissau, ingloriously called by the Portuguese colonialists until very recently an "overseas province." With this pompous name they tried to mask their presence as invaders in those lands and their relentless exploitation of the people.

My first encounter with Africa was not, however, with Guinea-Bissau but with Tanzania, to which, for a variety of reasons, I feel very closely related. I make this reference to underline how important it was for me to step for the first time on African soil, and to feel myself to be one who was returning and not one who was arriving. In truth, five years ago, as I left the airport of Dar es Salaam, going toward the university campus, the city opened before me as something I was seeing again and in which I reencountered myself. From that moment on, even the smallest things, like old acquaintances, began to speak to me of myself. The color of the skies; the blue-green of the sea; the coconut, the mango and the cashew trees; the perfume of the flowers; the smell of the earth; the bananas and, among them, my very favorite, the apple-banana; the fish cooked in coconut oil; the locusts hopping in the dry grass; the sinuous body movements of the people as they walked in the streets, their smiles so ready for life; the drums sounding in the depths of night; bodies dancing and, as they did so, "designing the world"; the presence among the people of expressions of their culture that the colonialists, no matter how hard they tried, could not stamp out —all of this took possession of me and made me realize that I was more African than I had thought.

Naturally, it was not only these aspects, considered by some people merely sentimental, that affected me. There was something else in that encounter: a reencounter with myself.

There is much I could say of the impressions that continue and of the learning I have done on successive visits to Tanzania. It is not this, however, that makes me refer now to this country to which I am so attached. I speak of Tanzania only to emphasize the importance for me of stepping on African soil and feeling as though I were returning somewhere, rather than arriving.

This sense of being at home on African soil was repeated, sometimes accentuated, when, in September of 1975, accompanied by the team from the Institute for Cultural Action (IDAC), I visited Guinea-Bissau for the first time, that is, when I "returned" to Guinea-Bissau.

In this introduction, I shall speak of what it has come to mean, not only to me but to the members of the team, as we participate in this rich and challenging experience in the field of education in general and, particularly, adult education, in which we are working *with* Guinean learners and educators, not working either *on* them, or simply *on their behalf.*

Before I do that, however, I should explain what led me to publish now, rather than later, the few letters I have written thus far to the Commissioner on Education and to the Coordinating Commission responsible for literacy education in Bissau. My basic intention is to offer readers, by means of the letters and of the introduction that precedes them, a dynamic vision of the activities being developed in that country and of the theoretical problems that underlie them. From this concept comes the title of the book, *Pedagogy in Process: The Letters to Guinea-Bissau.*

Between revealing the work as it progresses and publishing a book two or three years later as a final report, I prefer the former. If I should attempt another publication on the same experience, which I really hope to do, it will not be made up of the letters which I will continue to write. I prefer to feel as spontaneous in writing future letters as I did in preparing those now being published. This spontaneity—not a kind of neutrality —could be affected if, in writing future letters, I felt that I were working on a second volume of letters to Guinea-Bissau.

## Background and Assumptions of the Education Project

Given this explanation, let us begin to talk, without too much preoccupation with didactics, about the activities in Guinea. In doing this, I want to emphasize the satisfaction with which we, in the Department of Education of the World Council of Churches and the team of IDAC, received, in May of 1975, the official invitation of the government through the Commission on Education to make a first visit in order to discuss the bases of our collaboration in the field of literacy education for adults.

The struggle of the people of Guinea-Bissau and the Cape Verde Islands, under the extraordinary leadership of Amilcar Cabral and the comrades of PAIGC,* to expel the Portuguese colonizers was not in any way strange to us. We knew what this struggle had meant both for the formation of the political consciousness of the majority of the people and their leaders and also as a basic factor explaining the twenty-fifth of April in Portugal.†

We knew that we would be working not with cold, objective intellectuals, nor with neutral specialists, but with militants engaged in a serious effort at reconstruction of their country. I use the term "reconstruction" because Guinea-Bissau does not start from zero. Her cultural and historical roots are something very much her own, in the very soul of her people, which the violence of the colonialists could not destroy. She does, how-

---

*The African Party for the Independence of Guinea and the Cape Verde Islands (PAIGC).

†On April 25, 1974, a military coup overthrew the rightist dictatorship of the National Popular Action Party that had ruled Portugal for forty years.—Translator's note.

ever, start from zero with reference to the material conditions left by the invaders when, politically and militarily defeated in an impossible war, they had to abandon the country definitively after April twenty-fifth, leaving behind a legacy of problems and scarcities which spoke so eloquently of the "civilizing power" of colonialism.

For all of these reasons, we received the invitation with great satisfaction. It offered us an opportunity to participate, even minimally, in responding to the challenge posed by reconstruction.

We knew that we had something with which to meet that challenge. If that had not been true, there would be no explanation for our acceptance of the invitation. But, fundamentally, we knew that the help for which they asked would be true help only to the degree to which, in the process of offering it, we never pretended to be the exclusive Subjects of it, thus reducing the national leaders and people to being simply objects. Authentic help means that all who are involved help each other mutually, growing together in the common effort to understand the reality which they seek to transform. Only through such praxis—in which those who help and those who are being helped help each other simultaneously—can the act of helping become free from the distortion in which the helper dominates the helped. For this reason there can be no real help between dominating and dominated classes, nor between "imperial" and so-called "dependent" societies. These relationships can never be understood except in the light of class analysis.

It is for this reason that only as militants could we become true collaborators, even in a very small way—never as neutral specialists or as members of a foreign technical assistance mission. Our own political choices, and our praxis which is coherent with these choices, have kept us from even thinking of preparing in Geneva a project for the literacy education of adults with all of its points worked out in fine detail, to be taken to Guinea-Bissau as a generous gift. This project, on the contrary, together with the basic plans for our collaboration, would have to be born there, thought through by the national educators in harmony with the social situation in the country. Our cooperation in the design and practical application of the project would depend upon our ability to understand national reality; to deepen what we already knew about the liberation struggle and the experiments carried out by PAIGC in the older liberated zones, we began to read everything we could find, especially the works of Amilcar Cabral. These studies of ours, begun in Geneva, would be carried further in our first visit to the country and continued in subsequent visits if we should enter into a prolonged relationship. It would be in subsequent visits that we would think with the national educators in evaluation seminars about their own praxis. We would start, in any case, from a radical position, refusing to accept packaged or prefabricated solutions and avoiding every kind of cultural invasion, whether it be open or cleverly hidden.

Our political choice and its praxis also keeps us from even thinking that we could teach the educators and learners of Guinea-Bissau anything unless we were also learning with and from them. If the dichotomy between teaching and learning results in the refusal of the one who teaches to learn from the one being taught, it grows out of an ideology of domination. Those who are called to teach must first learn how to continue learning when they begin to teach.

Elza and I had had this experience—of learning first in order to continue learning—later as we were teaching. In our first meetings with Chilean educators, we listened much more than we spoke. When we did speak, it was in order to describe the praxis which was ours in Brazil—not to prescribe for Chilean educators but simply to present the negative and positive aspects of our experience. In learning with them and with the workers in the fields and factories, it became possible for us also to teach. If there was anything that we discovered in Brazil that we were able to repeat exactly in Chile, it was not to separate the act of teaching from the act of learning. We also learned not to attempt to impose on the Chilean context what we had done in different circumstances in Brazil. Experiments cannot be transplanted; they must be reinvented. One of our most pressing concerns when we were preparing as a team for our first visit to Guinea-Bissau was to guard against the temptation to overestimate the significance of some aspect of an earlier experience, giving it universal validity.

We tried to analyze our own experiences and those of others in different settings, giving increasing critical attention to the politics and ideology of literacy education for adults and of education in general. We also analyzed carefully the relation between literacy education, post-literacy and production within the total plan for the society. We looked at the relation between literacy education and general education. We sought a critical comprehension of the role that literacy education for adults might play in a society like that of Guinea, where people's lives had all been touched directly or indirectly by the war for liberation, "a cultural fact and a factor of culture," to use Amilcar Cabral's expression. The political consciousness of the people had been born of the struggle itself. While 90 percent of the people were illiterate, in the literal sense of the term, they were politically highly literate—just the opposite of certain communities which possess a sophisticated kind of literacy but are grossly illiterate about political matters.

These, then, were the central themes in our seminars during all of the time that we were preparing for our first visit to the country; they were also part of the concern of each one of us individually in our hours of personal reflection about our work in Guinea-Bissau. We never spent very long studying adult literacy methods and techniques for their own sake, but looked at them in relation to and in the service of a specific theory of knowledge, applied in practice, which in its turn must be consonant with a particular political stance. If the educator has a revolutionary stance and if his practice is coherent with that stance, then the learner in adult literacy education is one of the Subjects of the act of knowing. It becomes the duty of the educator to search out appropriate paths for the learner to travel and the best assistance that can be offered so that the learner is enabled to exercise the role of Subject in relation to learning during the process of literacy education. The educator must constantly discover and rediscover these paths that make it easier for the learner to see the object to be revealed, and finally learned, as a problem. The educator's task is not to use these means and these paths to uncover the object himself and to offer it, paternalistically, to the learner, thus denying him the effort of searching that is so indispensable to the act of knowing. Rather, in the connection between the educator and the learner, mediated by the object to be revealed, the most important factor is the development of a critical attitude *in relation to* the object and not a discourse by the educator *about* the object. And even when, in the midst of these relations, the educator and the learner come close to the object of their analysis and become curious about its meaning, they need the kind of solid information that is indispensable to accurate analysis. To know is not to guess; information is useful only when a problem has been posed. Without this basic problem-statement, the furnishing of information is not a significant moment in the act of learning and becomes simply the transfer of something from the educator to the learner.

From the beginning of my work in the field of adult literacy education, I have tried to get rid of little primers. Let me emphasize that it is the primers that I object to and not the other materials which help learners in their process of firming up and deepening their studies. I have always defended materials that help learners conquer language through the breaking up of generative words in order to construct other words through the various combinations of syllables. These materials involve a creative act and reinforce learning.

Unfortunately, this is not what happens, even with those primers whose authors, trying their best to go beyond the role of "donors," offer the learners opportunities to create words and short texts. Actually, much of the effort of the learners, especially in creating their own words, has already been programmed in the primers by their author. And so, instead of stimulating learners' curiosity, the primers reinforce a passive, receptive attitude which contradicts the creative act of knowing.

It seems to me that this is one of the problems in the field of education that a revolutionary society needs to address, that is, the meaning of the act of knowing. A revolutionary society should look at the roles that the act of knowing demands of its Subjects—creator, recreator, and reinventor. It should examine, also, the role of curiosity in relation to the object to be known: whether curiosity is related to the search for existing knowledge or to the attempt to create new knowledge. Such moments are, really, indivisible. The separation between these moments reduces the act of learning existing knowledge to mere bureaucratic transference. In such circumstances, the school, whatever its level, becomes a knowledge market; the professor, a sophisticated specialist who sells and distributes "packaged knowledge"; the learner, a client, who purchases and "consumes" this knowledge.

If the educator, on the other hand, is not bureaucratized in this process, but keeps his curiosity alive, the object is unveiled again for him or her, while the learner is in the process of unveiling it. Very often, the educator thus perceives a new dimension of that object which had, until now, been hidden.

It is essential that educators learning and learners educating make a constant effort to refuse to be bureaucratized. Bureaucracy annihilates creativity and transforms persons into mere repeaters of clichés. The more bureaucratized they become, the more likely they are to become alienated adherents of daily routine, from which they can never stand apart in order to understand their reason for being.

Coherence between the political-revolutionary stance of the educator and his/her action is the only way to avoid bureaucratization. The more vigilant the educator in living out this coherence, the more authentically militant s/he becomes, refusing, at the same time, the role of technician or specialist in some particular field.

It was, then, as militants, not as neutral specialists or cold technicians, that we accepted the invitation from the government of Guinea-Bissau. We left Geneva ready to see and hear, to inquire and to discuss. In our baggage we carried no saving plans or reports semiprepared.

As a team, we had talked in Geneva about the best way to see and hear, inquire and discuss so that the plan for our contribution might result—a plan for a program that would be born there, in dialogue with people of the country, about their own reality, their needs, and the possibility of our assistance. We could not design such a plan for them in Geneva.

We have never understood literacy education of adults as a thing in itself, as simply learning the mechanics of reading and writing, but, rather, as a political act, directly related to production, to health, to the regular system of instruction, to the overall plan for the society still to be realized. Therefore the process of seeing and hearing, questioning and discussing, would have to extend beyond the Commission on Education to other Commissions, to the Party, including the mass organizations. And so, our work plan for the first visit, merely outlined in Geneva, and actually developed in dialogue with national leaders in Guinea, had envisaged three major points of emphasis, never, of course, rigidly divided from each other.

## The First Emphasis: Learning History from the Commission on Education and Other Leaders

In the first phase of our visit, we entered into contact not only with the recently created Department of Adult Education, but with various teams of the Commission on Education.

We needed to know the central issues in primary and secondary schooling and the manner in which they were being addressed. We were interested in the modifications which had already been introduced in the general educational system inherited from the colonialists and in their potential for stimulating its gradual transformation. A new educational praxis, expressing different concepts of education consonant with the plan for the society as a whole, would be created by the Party with the people.

The inherited colonial education had as one of its principal objectives the de-Africanization of nationals. It was discriminatory, mediocre, and based on verbalism. It could not contribute anything to national reconstruction because it was not constituted for this purpose. Each level of the colonial system—primary, lycée, and technical—was separated from the preceding one. Schooling was antidemocratic in its methods, in its content, and in its objectives. Divorced from the reality of the country, it was, for this very reason, a school for a minority, and thus against the majority. It selected out only a very few of those who had access to it, excluded most of them after a few years and, due to continued selective filtering, the number rejected constantly increased. A sense of inferiority and of inadequacy was fostered by this "failure."[1]

This system could not help but reproduce in children and youth the profile that colonial ideology itself had created for them,[2] namely, that of inferior beings, lacking in all ability; their only salvation lay in becoming "white" or "black with white souls." The system, then, was not concerned with anything related closely to nationals (called "natives"). Worse than the lack of concern was the actual negation of every authentic representation of national peoples—their history, their culture, their language. The history of those colonized was thought to have begun with the civilizing presence of the colonizers. The culture of the colonized was a reflection of their barbaric way of seeing the world. Culture belonged only to the colonizers. The music of the colonized, their rhythm, their dance, the delicacy of their body movements, their general creativity—none of these had any value for the colonizers. And so these gifts were all repressed, and in their place the taste of the dominant metropolitan class was imposed. The alienating experience of colonial education was only counteracted for the colonized at those moments when, in an urge for independence, they rejected some of its aspects. At these times, the people "assumed their own history," inserting themselves into a process which could be called "the decolonizing of mentality" to which Aristides Pereira makes reference. Amilcar Cabral called it the "re-Africanization of mentality."

All of this implies a radical transformation of the educational system inherited from the colonizers. Such transformation can never be done mechanically. It requires a political decision coherent with the plan for the society to be created, and must be based on certain material conditions that also offer incentives for change. It demands increased production. At the same time it requires a reorientation of production through a new concept of distribution. A high degree of political clarity must underlie any discussions of what to produce, how to produce it, for what and for whom it is to be produced. Any change, even a change initiated timidly, in the interest of new material conditions in any significant aspect of society (such as, for example, in the dichotomy between manual and intellectual labor) necessarily provokes resistance from the old ideology that survives in the face of forces to create a new society.

Obviously these ideological resistances are the same ones that oppose the destruction of the incorrect notion that knowledge is something concluded, assuming for the educator the role of "possessor" of this completed knowledge that must be transferred to the learner who needs it. What is worse, the resistance is often not to the intellectual understanding of a concept of knowledge but to the action coherent with it. For this reason, the radical transformation of the educational system inherited from the colonizers requires an infrastructural effort. That is, it requires an effort toward massive change at the level of infrastructures and simultaneous action of an ideological nature. It implies the reorganization of the means of production and the involvement of workers in a specific form of education, through which they are called to become more than skilled production workers, through an understanding of the process of work itself.

In transforming the educational system inherited from the colonizers one of the necessary tasks is the training of new groups of teachers and the retraining of old ones. Among these teachers, and especially among those who have taught before, there will always be those who perceive themselves to be "captured" by the old ideology and who will consciously continue to embrace it; they will fall into the practice of undermining, either in a hidden or an open way, the new practice. From such persons one cannot hope for any positive action toward the reconstruction of society. But there will be others who, also perceiving themselves to be captive to the old ideology, will nonetheless attempt to free themselves from it through the new practice to which they will adhere. It is possible to work with these persons. They are the ones who "commit class suicide." The others refuse to do so.

Referring to the role of the middle class in the general picture of the struggle for national liberation, Amilcar Cabral affirmed: "If they are not to betray these objectives (of the liberation struggle), the middle class has only one possible road: that is, to strengthen their revolutionary conscience, to repudiate all that draws them toward middle-class standards and the natural attraction of that kind of class mentality, and to identify themselves with the working class by not opposing, in any way, the normal unfolding of the process of the revolution. This means that, in order to fulfill their specific revolutionary role in the struggle for national liberation, the revolutionary members of the middle class must be capable of committing suicide as a class in order to rise again as revolutionary workers, completely committed to the deepest aspirations of the people to which they belong.

"This alternative," Cabral goes on, "to betray the revolution or to commit class suicide, constitutes the real option of the middle class in the general picture of the struggle for national liberation."[3] The same alternatives exist today in the movement for national liberation which is the natural continuation of the liberation struggle.

These discussions about the subject of literacy education for adults cannot be understood apart from the problems to which we have just alluded briefly. This should not, of course, be taken to mean that literacy activities cannot begin until after the radical transformation of the system inherited from the colonizers has taken place. It does mean, however, that radical transformation, and not simply reform, is the objective to be pursued with clarity and speed.

The debate surrounding this fundamental problem—that of an educational system inherited from the colonial era—led us, necessarily, in our conversations with the team from the Commission on Education, to an analysis of another inheritance—that of the liberation war itself. This latter inheritance can be seen in the excellent experiments conducted in the older liberated zones, as they are now called, in areas of production and distribution, in the establishment of the new "peoples' markets" as well as in the fields of health, education and justice.

We wanted to know, above all, how those teams that were

preoccupied with the transformation of the inherited colonial system viewed this other inheritance, the war itself. The new system that would come into being could not be merely a fortuitous synthesis of the two inheritances but it must improve on and address at greater depth all that had been accomplished in the liberated zones, where an education, no longer elitist but eminently popular, had been developed.* In these areas, the local population had taken the matter of education into their own hands, just as they had done in supporting the guerilla fighters. A work school, closely linked to production and dedicated to the political education of the learners, had come into being in response to the real requirements of the liberation struggle. The children even had to learn what to do in order to live through the devastating attacks of enemy planes.

This was an education that not only expressed the climate of solidarity induced by the struggle itself, but also deepened it. Incarnating the dramatic present of the war, it both searched for the authentic past of the people and offered itself for their present.

Here, as in all of the dimensions of the liberation process, one can appreciate the prophetic vision of Amilcar Cabral. He had a capacity to analyze the reality of the country, never to deny it.

---

*"This educational work in the interior of the country had obtained important results, offering schooling for children over ten years of age. (Because of the war conditions, this had to be the minimum age for admission to primary schools.) In the academic year 1971–72, PAIGC had a total of 164 schools in the liberated zones where 258 teachers taught 14,531 students. Later, the best students were selected to attend live-in schools set up in neighboring countries by the Party. In addition, PAIGC was always very conscious of the requirements of national reconstruction and not merely of those created by the war with its need for young people in military service. Therefore particular attention was given to offering middle school and higher education to many groups of students. They were able to count on the support of nearby countries for this purpose and the result has been that a far larger number of Guinean students completed advanced courses during the war years than during the whole period of Portuguese occupation. In ten years under PAIGC more classes graduated than in five centuries of Portuguese domination. (In the ten years from 1963–73, the following cadres were graduated under PAIGC: 36 in higher education; 46 with the middle-level technical course; 241 with professional and specialized courses; and 174 with political and union courses. In comparison, from 1471 to 1961 only 14 Guineans finished higher education courses and 11 the technical level.)": Luiza Teotonio Pereira and Luis Motta, *Guiné Bissau—Três anos de Independência* (Lisbon, 1976), pp. 106–7.

He began always with what was actually true and not with what he might wish were true as he both denounced and announced. Denunciation and annunciation in Amilcar Cabral were never disassociated from each other, just as they were never outside the revolutionary praxis. From the midst of the struggle beside his comrades he denounced the oppressive reality of the exploitative colonialist farce that sought always to cover up its exploitation. In the same way he announced the new society that was being formed, deep in the heart of the old, through the revolutionary changes that were taking place. As with every person who truly lives out the coherence between political choice and actions, the word, for Cabral, was always a dialectical unity between action and reflection, practice and theory. He never allowed himself to be tempted on the one hand by empty words, nor on the other by activism.

His political clarity, the coherence between his choices and his practice, is at the root both of his refusal to be drawn into making undisciplined responses and of his rejection of manipulation. He dismissed any idea of the masses divided, following their own inclinations, marching in response to whatever happened, without a revolutionary party or leaders who could mobilize, organize and orient. In the same way he also rejected a leadership which felt that it "owned" the masses. Unlimited freedom and bureaucratic authoritarianism were equally abhorrent. Neither a leadership which followed the masses so far behind that they got lost in the dust stirred up by the people, nor leaders so far out in front that they left the people enshrouded in their dust, but leaders always *with* the people, teaching and learning mutually in the liberation struggle—this was his way. Like Guevara and like Fidel, Cabral was in constant communion with the people, whose past he knew so well and in whose present he was so deeply rooted, a present filled with struggle, to which he gave himself without restriction. He could thus see the future before others did. In each of the days that he lived so intensely, there was always a possible dream, a viable history that could begin to be forged on that very day.

Once when he was discussing the magical powers of amulets with some soldiers, he said, "We will not die if we do not make war or if we do not attack the enemy at the point of his vulnerability. But if we make mistakes, if we find ourselves in a position of weakness, we will die; there is no other way out. You will say to me: 'Cabral does not know, but we have seen various cases in which it was an amulet that saved one of our comrades from death. The bullets came and were deflected.' You may say that. I hope that the sons of our sons, when they hear such stories and when they rejoice that PAIGC was able to direct the struggle in accord with the reality of the country, will say, 'Our fathers struggled hard but they believed in some very strange things.' What I am saying to you perhaps does not make sense now. I will speak again tomorrow. . . ."[4]

Amilcar Cabral knew that cannons alone do not make a war and that the resolution of a war only comes when the vulnerability of the oppressed becomes strength, capable of transforming the power of the oppressor into weakness. This was the source of his constant concern, the patient impatience with which he invariably gave himself to the political and ideological formation of militants, whatever their level or the sector in which they were active. This was also the source of the special attention which he dedicated to the work of education in the liberated zones and also of the tenderness he showed when, before going into battle, he visited the children in the little schools, sharing in their games and always having just the right word to say to them. He called them the "flowers of our revolution."

We were not really surprised, therefore, at the clarity with which the national teams analyzed all of these points. The Commissioner on Education was present in these sessions and felt himself very much part of the process in which everyone was conscious of the significance of recreating a society. They knew well the obstacles that confronted them daily—from the lack of the most minimal material things, a typewriter for instance, to the overwhelming need to train leadership groups in the most diverse fields in order to put all of their projects in practice.

We were able to observe Commissioner Mario Cabral's lucid comprehension of the rich educational experience developed during the war as well as the positive way in which he faced the radical transformation of the inherited system. He knew all the time that the change could not take place through magic. Mario Cabral was aware, as a result of his militant leadership of the Commission on Education, that the relations between the educational system and the total society are dialectic in nature and not mechanical. Recognizing the limits of formal education as a subsystem within a larger system, he also recognized its fundamental role in the formation of a new mentality, coherent with the objectives of the new society to be created. He knew, further, that this fundamental role could not be realized if, instead of dealing with the social practice in the country, he tried to create an education to fit the future society now being formed. Such an attempt would be highly idealistic and could not, for that very reason, become a reality. Between the alternatives of abruptly closing all the schools inherited from the colonial era, at both the primary and middle-school levels, while the educational system was being entirely reoriented, and that of introducing into the old system some fundamental reforms capable of accelerating the future radical transformation consistent with the changes operating in the material bases of the society, he preferred the latter.

It was imperative to reformulate the programs of geography, history and the Portuguese language, changing all the reading texts that were so heavily impregnated with the colonialist ideology. It was an absolute priority that Guinean students should study their own geography and not that of Portugal, the inlets of the sea and not the Rio Tejo. It was urgent that they study their history, the history of the resistance of their people to the invader and the struggle for their liberation which gave them back the right to make their own history, and not the history of the kings of Portugal and the intrigues of the court. It was necessary that Guinean students be called to participate in the efforts toward national reconstruction and not to "exercises in clay modeling of the blind poet crowned in laurels."[5] And it was also important to begin, perhaps timidly at first, to bring about the first steps toward a closeness between the middle-school students of Bissau and productive work.

"The school in the country" was one of the projects about which Mario Cabral spoke to us. It involved temporarily moving urban schools with their teachers and students to rural areas where, living in camps, they might learn with the peasants through participation in productive activities and also teach them some things, without in any way eliminating their regular school activities.

Thus experiments were begun in 1975 which would later be extended in 1976, to integrate productive labor with the normal school activities, with the intention of combining work and study so that, as far as possible, the former might provide direction for the latter and that, together, they might form a unity.

To the degree to which these experiments are systematized and deepened, it is possible, increasingly, to derive from productive activities the programmatic content of the different disciplines which, in the traditional system, were "transferred" verbally to the students, if anything happened at all.

In a certain moment it becomes true that one no longer studies in order to work nor does one work in order to study; one studies in the process of working. There comes about, thus, a true unity between practice and theory. We must be clear, however, that what is eliminated is not that study which is critical reflection on practice completed or in process (theory), but the separation between the two. The unity of theory and practice thus establishes the unity, also, between the school, whatever its level, and productive activity as a dimension of the concrete context.

In spite of the difficulties that the Commission has faced, some of an ideological nature, such as the resistance of students who did not accept the idea of working with their hands, and some of a material nature, such as the lack of transportation, it is possible to list a number of very positive experiences, such as: the work, on Sunday mornings in the state granaries, of 120 students who were just completing their middle-school course; the participation of students from the second and third years of middle school in Bissau in the productive work in the gardens of the Institute of Friendship; two months of work by the second-year students of the Salvador Allende School in the area of cattle raising; and the gardens planted by a very large number of primary school children in the capital.

It is important to point out that before and after these trips to the country, the middle-school students met with agricultural technicians to discuss various aspects of the activities in which they would be engaged. The technicians also accompanied them on these trips. In evaluation seminars on their return, their understanding of the points addressed in the preparatory meetings was either confirmed, deepened or corrected.

The openness of the peasants who received the visiting urban students and their readiness both to teach and to learn are also very significant. Basically, however, it was probably the urban students who learned most from their first experience of intimate relationship with the hard work of tilling the soil, harvesting and producing.

These experiments took place not only in Bissau where the difficulties are greater, but in other parts of the country with more favorable conditions. At the present time these experiments have been extended to include almost the whole country. Some schools, like the middle school in Bafatá, have two fields of agriculture. The schools of the older liberated zones continue to be self-sufficient through the productive work of their teachers and students. Actually, in the Bafatá region 96 of the 106 schools have some agricultural work.

Measures such as these are the precursors of much more profound change. The Commission on Education has allied itself with these efforts, avoiding, however, any attempt at rigid centralization. At the time of our visit, two Cuban educators were closely related to the work which had just been begun in the area of training and retraining of teachers. I shall be speaking more later of all of these transformations, which are now taking place.

## Activities Already Taking Place in the Field of Adult Literacy

Two basic initiatives have already been undertaken in the field of adult literacy education—one related to the Armed Forces of the People (FARP) and the other to the Commission on Education which has just created a Department of Adult Education.

There is evident a movement toward the unification of these two efforts, indispensable for the efficiency of a national program. However, the unique characteristics of each will be respected.

It is interesting to note that literacy education, whether from the point of view of FARP or of the Commission on Education, has been seen as a political act in which the learners, with the help of enablers, engage in a critical approach to reading and writing and not in an alienating and mechanical memorization of syllables, words and sentences which are given to them. This position, of course, is in complete accord with our own. The problem is not at the level of conceptualization but, rather, in making the process concrete.

The most important factor in the literacy education of adults is not the learning of reading and writing, which may result in the reading of texts without any critical comprehension of the social context to which they refer. This is the kind of literacy which interests the dominant classes when, for different reasons, they see some need to stimulate among the dominated classes "their first entry into the world of letters." The more "neutral" this "entry," the better it pleases those with power.

In a revolutionary context, on the contrary, it is important that the learners perceive, or deepen their perception, that the most important thing for them is to make history and to be made and remade by it, and not to read alienating stories. Running the risk of appearing schematically symmetrical, I would say that, in the first case, the learners are never called to think critically about the conditioning of their own thought process; to reflect on the reason for their own present situation; to make a new "reading" of the reality that is presented to them simply as something to which they should adapt themselves. The thought-language, absurdly separated from objectivity, and the mechanisms used to interject the dominant ideology, are never discussed. They learn that knowledge is something to be "consumed" and not made and remade. Illiteracy is sometimes thought of as a harmful weed and, at other times, as an illness. Thus people speak of its "eradication" or refer to it as a "plague."

Existing as objects in the general context of class society, oppressed and forbidden to *be,* illiterates continue as objects in the process of learning to read and write. They are brought to the learning process, not as persons invited to know the knowledge of the past so that, recognizing its limitations, they can know more. On the contrary, what is proposed for them is the passive acceptance of packaged knowledge.

In the revolutionary perspective, the learners are invited to think. Being conscious, in this sense, is not simply a formula or a slogan. It is a radical form of being, of being human. It pertains to beings that not only know, but know that they know. The act of learning to read and write, in this instance, is a creative act that involves a critical comprehension of reality. The knowledge of earlier knowledge, gained by the learners as a result of analyzing praxis in its social context, opens to them the possibility of new knowledge. The new knowledge, going far beyond the limits of the earlier knowledge, reveals the reason for being behind the facts, thus demythologizing the false interpretations of these same facts. And so, there is now no more separation between thought-language and objective reality. The reading of a text now demands a "reading" within the social context to which it refers.

In this sense, literacy education for adults becomes an introduction to the effort to systematize the knowledge that rural and urban workers gain in the course of their daily activity—a knowledge that is never self-explanatory but must always be understood in terms of the ends that it serves. This process of systematization deepens in the stages that follow literacy.

Parallel with the reorganization of the means of production, an essential task for critical understanding and attention in a revolutionary society is the valorization—and not the idealization—of popular wisdom that includes the creative activity of a people and reveals the levels of their knowledge regarding reality. What is implied is not the transmission to the people of a knowledge previously elaborated, a process that ignores what they already know, but the act of returning to them, in an organized form, what they have themselves offered in a disorganized form.* In other words, it is a process of knowing with the people how they know things and the level of that knowledge. This means challenging them, through critical reflection, regarding their own practical experience and the ends that motivate them in order, in the end, to organize the findings, and thus to replace mere opinion about facts with an increasingly rigorous understanding of their significance. This is the challenge to which Amilcar Cabral gave so much attention when, analyzing the liberation struggle as both "a cultural fact and a factor of culture," he emphasized the necessity for this culture to become increasingly more scientific, in the truest sense of that term, thus overcoming what he called the "weaknesses of culture."

A work such as this, based always on the practice of thinking about practice, through which practice is perfected, might give rise to true study centers which, although they revolved around certain specific themes such as agriculture or health, for example, could develop global analyses of these themes. Such centers, through their ongoing task of systematizing and deepening knowledge, might become units of a future university—a type of university that grows from and with the working classes and is not imposed on them, which, in the end, always means that it is *against* them.

The most important feature of such work with the people is the exercise of a critical stance in the face of reality. Reality itself thus becomes the object of knowledge—understood by means of analysis of the action that transforms it. Every day, practical activity becomes a permanent object of study. The understanding that results is far more significant than the immediate utilitarian purpose of the activity itself. Thus, activity becomes not only a source of knowledge about itself and its own rationale, but also a means of comprehending other matters related to it.

The question posed for a revolutionary society is not only one of how to train workers in the skills considered necessary to increase production—skills that in a capitalist society are in-

---

*"We must teach the masses with precision what we receive from them with confusion," said Mao in an interview with André Malraux (*Antimémoires* [Paris, 1967], p. 531).

creasingly more limited in scope—but one of enlarging the workers' horizons through an understanding of the productive process itself.

But let us speak now of what was actually happening in the field of literacy education for adults at the time of our first visit.

As might be expected, the high level of political clarity among the members of the People's Armed Forces (FARP) had already meant that their work met with extremely positive results in spite of the innumerable difficulties that had to be overcome. Some of these difficulties were material in nature. Others arose from a lack of efficiency among certain literacy workers who expected immediate permanent change and perfection as a result of their efforts.

In July 1975, two months before our first visit to the country and following a training course that had been, initially, under the direction of one leader,* 82 literacy workers and seven supervisors from FARP were already active in the military installations in Bissau while 150 others were completing their training.

The FARP project, conceived by the Political Commissioner of the Armed Forces, Julio de Carvalho, and his assistants, included three integrated phases. The first was an intensive effort at literacy by means of which they sought to overcome the problem of illiteracy among the military in the Bissau zone as rapidly as possible. In the second phase, parallel with the initiation of post-literacy work in Bissau, literacy education was to be extended to all of the military units in the country. In the third and final phase, FARP would "overflow its own borders" in order to, in the words of Julio de Carvalho, reach the whole civilian population. This "overflowing" would be carried out by military personnel who, although they were engaged in productive labor and no longer officially in the army, would remain linked to FARP, and by some still in the military especially assigned to literacy work among civilians.

At the time of writing this introduction, I can verify that the

---

*This leader had participated in a seminar in Lisbon, coordinated by Professor Cintra, in which the fundamental aspects of the author's work in Brazil were analyzed.

first two phases are under way. Post-literacy work has begun in the military installations in Bissau—where there is practically no illiteracy remaining—and the expansion of literacy education has reached 80 percent of the total armed forces in the rest of the country. The third phase is in its beginning stages. All of these efforts are in addition to the collaboration of representatives of FARP with the Coordinating Commission for Adult Literacy of which they are also members. This is the commission that, in accordance with the policies of the Government and of the Party, plans and supervises adult literacy work in the civilian population.

Obviously it was necessary that the five members of our team* should be divided in order to visit at least some of the Culture Circles in action. At the stage at which we found ourselves—that of seeing and listening, asking and discussing, it was essential for us to observe how things were going in the Circles, among the participants and the literacy workers. We wanted to see both the creative aspects of their work and those instances where, on the contrary, they might be engaged merely in repetition and memorization. We were eager to know whether the learners had been able to appropriate for themselves their own "word," developing an ability to express themselves as conscious participants in a political act, or whether they were simply learning to read and write.

It is important to note that our attitude in visiting the Culture Circles was neither that of persons inclined to overestimate what we were seeing, nor were we like those so attached to ideal models that they cannot see the distance between those ideals and concrete reality. We felt neither uncontained euphoria in the face of good work nor negativity regarding the mistakes that we might encounter. What was important was to see what might really be happening under the limited material conditions we knew existed. We wanted to discover what could be done better under these conditions and, if this were not possible, to consider ways to improve the conditions themselves.

---

*At the time of the visit, the team was made up of Miguel D'Arcy de Oliveira, Claudius Ceccon, Marcos Arruda, Elza Freire and Paulo Freire. Later, two persons living in Bissau, José Barbosa and Gisèle Ouvray, and another in Geneva, Rosisca D'Arcy de Oliveira, were added.

What we discovered in the Culture Circles was that, in spite of some difficulties and errors, the learners and workers were engaged in an effort that was preponderantly creative. Much more than the mastery of the mechanics of reading and writing was going on. This was the important fact.

Among the most obvious errors, we might note the impatience of some of the workers that led them to create the words instead of challenging the learners to do so for themselves; the tendency of some to rely on the repetition of syllables in chorus; or the lack of vivacity on the part of some of the workers as they participated in discussions of the themes related to the generative words.

The lack of such mistakes would really have surprised us, especially since the time given to training and theoretical formation of the workers had been so short. The ongoing process of the evaluation seminars would be a powerful force in overcoming these mistakes. Effective practices would be reinforced and errors eliminated.

We want to note the creative imagination that we were able to observe in many of the workers. One of them, for example, arrived at the meeting place of the Culture Circle, greeted the learners and immediately began to sweep the classroom with an old broom. Patiently he moved from one corner of the room to the other, stopping sometimes to look under the benches on which the learners, already beginning to show signs of impatience, were seated. They could not understand their teacher's behavior, nor the thoroughness with which he pursued his task of sweeping what seemed to them an already clean room. Finally, one of them, expressing what all were wondering, asked, "Comrade, when will we begin our class?"

"The class began as soon as you arrived," replied the teacher, asking immediately, "What have I been doing?"

"Cleaning the room," they replied.

"Exactly," said the teacher. Going to the improvised blackboard, he wrote: "CLEAN." "That is the word that we will study today, 'CLEAN.' "

The educator is a politician and an artist who must use the

science of techniques but must never become a cold, neutral technician.

If our attitude in visiting the Culture Circles had been one of the two referred to above—easy euphoria in the face of what was effective or negativity in the face of mistakes—we might have idealized all that we saw or decreed the whole experiment invalid. In either case, we would have been wrong.

In the most populous sections of Bissau, in the experiments in work with civilians, the situation was completely different, but, at the same time, completely understandable. It is one thing to work with FARP, where the militants possess great clarity about the significance of national reconstruction and the continuation of the struggle because of their participation in the long pursuit of liberation. It is quite another to work in crowded areas of the city where the people were not touched in any direct way by the war but, rather, were deeply influenced by the colonialist ideology. Thus, while there were 82 functioning Culture Circles among the military in Bissau at the time of our first visit, everything among the civilians still remained to be started, or, in many cases, to be done over.

What both of these experiments—within FARP and in the populous neighborhoods of Bissau—made very clear was the need for establishing priorities in the literacy program for adults. Although the objectives were national in scope, the program must start in certain predetermined areas on the basis of the clearest possible criteria. If literacy efforts were to achieve their primary objective, that of contributing effectively to national reconstruction, then it would also be necessary to establish a dynamic relation between them and all of the other forms of social intervention in any way related to or dependent upon literacy. Literacy education for adults, like all other forms of education, cannot be imposed on the social practice of a society but must emerge from this practice as one of its dimensions.

There would be no sense in transforming the emerging National Literacy Program for Adults into just one more campaign of the traditional type that we all know so well. Either through ingenuousness or artifice, all of these campaigns idealize literacy and give it a power that it does not, in itself, possess. The question facing the Guineans is not that of whether to do literacy education for its own sake or to do it as a means of transformation but, rather, how to put it at the service of national reconstruction.

For these reasons, literacy education should become concrete through projects in areas where, in accordance with the policies of the Party carried out by the government, certain changes in the social relations of production are either already taking place or about to be initiated. The second important area is within the various administrative organs of the State—hospitals, postal services, public works agencies—where literacy education might enable employees to engage in other new tasks demanded by national reconstruction.* Mario Cabral emphasized the great need for a close relation between the Commission on Education and those responsible for planning, for agriculture and for health. Cooperation with the mass organizations of the Party, such as African Youth Amilcar Cabral (JAAC) whose members are already doing valuable work in the area of literacy, can also contribute to joint efforts in behalf of national reconstruction.

We made contact with all of these organizations and commissions in the first phase of our visit, as well as with the Political Commission of FARP to which we have already made reference. We were received in a visit that was more for work than for protocol by Comrade Francisco Mendes, the Chief Commissioner, and by the President of the Council of State, Luiz Cabral.

We were particularly interested in the possible contribution of the Commission on Information in future programs of literacy education. They clearly understand information in the dynamic sense of developing communication rather than simply the transmission of messages. Through the use of radio, newspapers and other channels they could assist in the important task of mobilizing large numbers of people for active participation in literacy efforts.

---

*While these matters were discussed briefly on our first visit, they were more central to our discussions in the second visit, in February of 1976 when they became more clearly defined.

Our conversations with responsible persons in the Commissions on Health and Agriculture were naturally more brief than those with the Commission on Education, but they helped us to see the necessary interdependence of literacy and health and agricultural production. Preventive medicine and the encouragement of mutual help in the development of cooperatives and on State farms appeared as significant educational concerns that were basic to all of the Commissions in their dedication to the goals of development for the country.

Therefore, a major question confronting the Commission on Education, as the Commissioner so lucidly pointed out, is the inclusion of all of these concerns in adult-literacy projects. At the same time that students are learning reading and writing, they can, for example, consider their own practices with regard to the mosquito and the battle against malaria. Militant workers in production cooperatives, when they serve as literacy workers, can share their own experience regarding the advantages of mutual assistance in the accomplishment of work over individual efforts as the basis for establishing new cooperatives. In effective adult literacy education there is no place for exclusive categories of working and learning. The concerns of all of the different Commissions meet in the life of the people and can be incorporated into their process of learning and growing.

Visual materials based on the experience of other African countries and accompanied by analyses that transcend geographical barriers can also be used to give people a broader vision of reality. To consider the fight against mosquitoes in a rural area of Guinea-Bissau, and then to see the same situation in a rural community in Mozambique, Tanzania or Saõ Tomé e Principe, would offer an opportunity not only to think about this problem itself but to consider other problems in relation to the experience of these countries.

## The Second Emphasis: Visits to the Older Liberated Zones

The second phase of our first stay in Guinea-Bissau was dedicated to rapid visits to some of the older liberated zones. It was here that PAIGC, as I mentioned earlier, had carried out some

highly important experiments in education, health, justice, production and distribution, the latter through the "People's Markets" that succeeded, in the space of only one year after the total
independence of the country, in gaining control of commerce.[6]

Although in part influenced by bad weather, these visits were
able to give us many important contacts with local political
commissions. We heard of their experiences during the struggle
and of the things they had learned from them, leading not only
to their survival and the defeat of the enemy forces but to their
commitment to apply that learning in the continuation of that
same struggle in the movement for national reconstruction. We
made contact also with many technicians, both national and
foreign, and with a number of primary-school teachers participating in a first training seminar based on the teaching principles of Freinet.*

It was, however, not until our second visit to the country in
February 1976 that we were able to deepen our understanding
of the situation in the interior, both through more extensive
travels in rural areas and through conversations with students
and peasants.

In any case, I would like to record here at least one of the
incidents that occurred in one of those visits, touching us very
deeply. Elza and I had a remarkable conversation with the
young director of a live-in school. He spoke softly, coolly and
objectively. He told pieces of a history that, in one sense, he had
made, and by which he had also been shaped. Without rhetoric
or the exaggerated use of adjectives, and also without cold
impartiality, he described to us, in a profoundly human manner,
the work of his school in a liberated zone. He spoke of the way
that the school and the community were integrated in the common task of sustaining the struggle, the task assigned to them
by PAIGC, to conquer and drive out the invader and to liberate
the country. He referred to Amilcar Cabral, neither sentimen-
tally nor as a mythological figure to be worshipped, but as a
symbol, a significant presence in the history of his people.

---

*Celestin Freinet, a French educator, born in 1896.

It was not necessary for him to use the terms "symbol" or "significant presence" for me to realize that it was in this way that he saw Cabral. This feeling is general in Guinea-Bissau and the Cape Verde Islands, the result of the authenticity of the great leader's witness and of the intensity of his communion with the people, without which he could not have accomplished what he did nor been what he was and continues to be for his people. No one can live completely alone. Long before Cabral became the "Father of the Nation," he was the "Son of the People" who learned with them and taught them in the revolutionary praxis.*

While the young worker was talking with Elza and me of the experience of the school, of the students and teachers working and learning together, including how to defend themselves against the cruel enemy bombardments, the role that that experience has played and continues to play in the struggle for national reconstruction became increasingly clear to us. We could also discern its role in replacing the old educational system inherited from the colonizers.

During the whole time that we were together, waiting out a severe rainstorm on the narrow porch of a tiny house, we listened much more than we spoke. Once in a while we asked a question that enabled the young educator to clarify what he had said or to remember some other incident.

"We always had, not far from the school, shelters where we could accommodate the children and people from the surrounding area in case of enemy attack," he said. "As soon as they began to hear the sound of the planes, everyone began to organize, rapidly and almost instinctively, to abandon the area. Everyone knew what to do—and did it—on those occasions. One time," he continued, "when we returned from hiding, after an attack, we found three of our comrades lying in the courtyard

---

*In this connection we remember an incident referred to by President Luiz Cabral. At the time of Amilcar Cabral's assassination by the colonialists, a militant who stood beside his fallen body said, "I do not cry for Comrade Cabral. He has not died. The one who speaks now is not I, but he. He speaks through me. Comrade Cabral will continue to speak through his people, calling us for the battle and for the victory against the oppressor."

of the school, their stomachs cut open. Two were already dead. One was dying. With them were three fetuses, pierced through with a bayonet."

I did not ask him how the authors of such a crime had arrived in the liberated zone. I did not care whether they had come by a plane landing in a field after the bombing or whether they were soldiers of one of the advance guards of the colonialist army. None of this interested me at that moment. I could only ask, as my hands trembled, what they did when they succeeded in capturing so depraved an assassin.

I had the impression that the young man perceived in my tone of voice, in my trembling hands, in my face, in my whole being, and in Elza's look and her silence which cried aloud, the immense sense of revulsion which had come over us.

His voice still soft and gentle, his reply was a teaching in itself. "Evil persons like that," he said, "when they are caught, are punished in accord with the people's judgment. The revolution punishes but it does not torture. Comrade Cabral always spoke of the respect that we should show to the enemy. That was a rule of our party and of PAIGC."

And this is a radical difference between the violence of the oppressor and the violence of the oppressed. That of the former is exercised in order to express the violence implicit in exploitation and domination. That of the latter is used to eliminate violence through the revolutionary transformation of the reality that makes it possible.

The political maturity revealed by that young militant and brought about by the liberation struggle as a "cultural fact and a factor of culture" is a constant in Guinea-Bissau with the exception of a few sectors of the population in certain areas less affected by the struggle itself. In Guinea-Bissau they speak of the struggle without oratorical tirades or excesses. They speak of what it taught, of what it required; of what it continues to teach and to demand as part of an ongoing process. They speak of the engagement it implies and of the vigilance it demands.

In truth, this simplicity and absence of triumphalism reveal, on the one hand, a deeply rooted sense of security; on the other, a true humility that, for this very reason, does not spend itself in false modesty. Security and humility were formed in the difficult struggle overcoming obstacles, and in the victory over the enemy. It is because the people are so deeply rooted in this security and humility that one perceives the firm commitment of both the people and their leaders to make concrete the dream that they have pursued since the beginning of the struggle—to reinvent their society, banishing the exploitation of some by others, and overcoming injustices.

Discreetly, with revolutionary modesty and, coherent with this modesty, absolute assurance of the historic role of his people, the young militant spoke to Elza and me of the praxis in which he had been remade and continued to be remade, together with his comrades. And he spoke of the joy of having participated in the hardships of the struggle, of the joy in his involvement in the reconstruction of his country.

On the return trip to Bissau, looking from the window of the helicopter piloted by two Soviet citizens together with two young nationals learning from them, I saw spread below us the foliage of the trees burned by napalm.

I looked intently and with curiosity. There was not one animal. A few large birds flew calmly by. I remembered what President Luiz Cabral had said to us in our first meeting when he spoke, with the same seriousness displayed by the young school director, about different incidents in the struggle. "There was a time," said the President, "when the animals of Guinea all sought 'asylum' in neighboring countries. Only the small monkeys stayed behind, taking refuge in the liberated zones. They were deathly afraid of the 'tuga.'* In the end the poor things feared us, too. That was because we found ourselves forced to eat them. I hope that very soon all of our animals will return, convinced that the war is over."

From the window of the helicopter, I looked intently, curiously. There was not yet a sign, at least in that part of the country, of that return.

Back in Bissau, while our team prepared for the last phase of

---

*A term used in Guinea-Bissau to refer to "white-faced" people.—Translator's note.

the visit, there was an event that affected us profoundly. Since I have referred to it so many times since then, I cannot omit it here.

It was a warm September morning. The heat was almost suffocating. The celebration of the anniversary of independence was in progress.

Deep inside a large park was a huge platform on which the national authorities, the foreign diplomats, special guests, and delegations from foreign countries were seated.

A wide variety of groups were in the parade, representing popular organizations from the different sections of Bissau. Children, young people, women and men were all colorfully dressed. They sang and danced. All was in movement. They came and went, curving and recurving in an extraordinary richness of rhythm. The whole multitude along the avenue that opened into the park participated actively in the parade. They were not there only to see and hear, but to express, consciously, the joy of being there as a people who had won the right to *be*.

The multitude sang and moved together. This was not, in any sense, a folkloric spectacle watched by a few people at a distance. Rather, it was a festival. Everyone was living a very important day.

The parade concluded with the review of units of FARP and then the President, Luiz Cabral, began his discourse. Directly in front of the platform where he stood, a group from the military band was drawn up at attention. At a certain moment, one of the soldiers in the band, as though he were falling on top of himself, fainted. The President stopped his speech. He looked fixedly at the soldier who was being supported by his comrades. The crowd perceived what was happening. They opened a path for a car that approached and, in a moment, took the soldier to the hospital. The President watched the car until it disappeared. Only then did he continue to speak.

At my side, in a very low voice, Elza said, "This was the most beautiful moment of our visit to this country. We really have much to learn from a people who live so intensely the unity between word and deed. The individual here is valued as a person. The human person is something concrete and not an abstraction."

The President continued with his discourse. Everything about him was authentic. His word was for the people. How coherent his action was with his word in the face of the incident which had occurred! It had taken only a few seconds, yet many years of struggle explained it. That was certainly not the first time that Luiz Cabral, the militant, expressed, in whatever form, his solidarity with a companion in difficulty. Luiz Cabral, the President, stopped his speech and, very worried, accompanied with his eyes the comrade who had fainted on that hot September morning; Luiz Cabral, the soldier, must have stopped innumerable times to attend a comrade fallen in the common struggle for the liberation of their people.

Incidents like this, whose profound meaning is indisputable, are not isolated or extraordinary events in Guinea-Bissau. They constitute a way of life for the people. It would have been strange if the President, "distant and cold," had continued his discourse when his comrade of FARP had been taken ill.

What seems of fundamental importance to me is that the values born in the duress of struggle continue to prevail. The more conscious that PAIGC, as the vanguard of the people, is of the necessity of preserving its communion with the people, in whose hearts their very position as vanguard is sealed, the more surely the revolution will be safe from threats of distortion. The degree to which it seeks to preserve and develop its oneness with the working classes will determine the understanding of "class suicide" born so long ago in the thought of Amilcar Cabral.[7] If this "suicide" gets lost, it will open the way for the return to power of a "bureaucratized bourgeoisie" separated from the working classes even when it claims to speak in their name.

## The Third Emphasis: Making Plans for Future Collaboration

I said in the beginning of this introduction that our work plan, outlined in Geneva and fully elaborated with our colleagues in Guinea-Bissau, had divided our time in the country into three basic phases, never really separate one from the other. The first two, which I sought to characterize as times of seeking to see and hear, question and discuss, were actually analytical in nature. The third phase—synthesis—grew naturally from them. In fact, this latter activity was taking place all the time even in the midst of analysis, from which it can never really be separated. It is for this reason that much of what happened in the third phase of the visit has already been described, although somewhat tentatively, in what I have said about the first two analytical phases. During these, taking as far as possible the reality of the country as a whole as the object of our curiosity, we tried to separate it into its several parts in order to know it better.

During the synthesis, being formed, as I said before, within the analysis itself, our effort was to bring together again the separated parts. Basically, the two actions are integrated in one dynamic movement that includes taking the object apart and putting it back together again.

In the first two phases, we looked on reality as a code that we were trying to decipher, sometimes with the national groups and sometimes among ourselves as a visiting team during our evaluation meetings while the work was in process. In this latter instance, we sometimes were engaged in a double task. Sometimes we took reality itself as the object of our analysis, attempting to "read it" critically. At other times, the object of our reflection was the process in which we had been engaged with the national teams when, with them, we had sought to analyze reality. In this way, we were analyzing the earlier analysis, trying to recapture critically the way in which we had perceived the same reality as the object of our curiosity.

Naturally, while we were participants in the same process of decoding reality in dialogue with the national teams, we could not, on the one hand, be mere silent spectators nor, on the other, be the exclusive Subjects of the act of decoding. It would have been contradictory to the basic principles underlying our trip to Guinea-Bissau to assume that we were the exclusive Subjects of the decoding of reality while living out the role of receivers of the decoding (carried out, in this case, by the national teams) and then, at the last moment of synthesis, to offer our interpretation, almost mysteriously, as a kind of zealously guarded, secret revelation.

Actually, we found ourselves involved with the national teams in an act of knowing in which we, as much as they, had to assume the role of knowing Subjects. The dialogue between us and the national teams, mediated by the reality that we were seeking to know, was the seal of that act of knowing. It would be through knowing and reknowing together that we would begin to learn and to teach together also.

I underline this point not only as something that should be said in the sequence of this introduction, but in order that, once again, I can make clear my position—not always clearly understood—that dialogue authenticates both the act of knowing and the role of the knowing Subject in the midst of the act.

This was, moreover, a rich theme that we debated and sought to deepen at the very beginning of our visit, principally in our study meetings with Mario Cabral and his teams from the Commission on Education. It was one to which we returned in our successive visits to the country. This theme was referred to, often rather fully, at the beginning of this essay and, for that very reason, it could not be omitted here.

Dividing the third phase of our visit in two parts, we saved the first part to work with Mario Cabral and his assistants on the recapitulation of our earlier effort, carried out together, to analyze reality—the decoding of which we had been able to accomplish.

The recapitulation, which it was our task to initiate, meant that we must make clear the "reading" which we had made of national reality. Our "reading," in its turn, was put before the teams of the Commission on Education as a new challenge to which they must respond—either accepting it or rejecting it, totally or in part, improving it or deepening it. In the synthesis, we thus returned to the analysis, in order to reach a new synthesis.

At the conclusion of the final phase of our visit, we discussed with the national leaders the bases for our continuing contribution to the work since this had been requested by the Commissioner, Mario Cabral, on behalf of the government and with the agreement of the Party. We were able at this point to base our discussions on what we had seen and heard firsthand, on the replies made to our inquiries, and on our common understand-ing of the role of education in general and of literacy education in particular in the process of national reconstruction.

In essence, the project that we outlined called for some activi-ties to be carried out in Geneva and others that we would ac-complish in Guinea-Bissau. Three visits were agreed to for 1976 —all of which were realized. It was also agreed that a member of the IDAC team would be located in Bissau, without any expense to the government, to work full time for the Coordinat-ing Commission for Adult Literacy. This plan has also been in effect since February 1976. The Commission itself was created by Mario Cabral as a result of our meetings during the first visit.

It was further agreed that we would evaluate the activities going on in the field of adult literacy on the basis of reports to be sent during the intervals between our visits to the country. As part of this process, we would continue to probe more deeply some of the aspects central to our discussions during the first visit.

The methods of work in subsequent visits to the country would be substantially the same as those adopted in the first visit: a period of analysis, in the dynamic sense of the term as I described it above, and a period of synthesis from which would result the need for new analysis.

In Geneva we would continue to deepen our understanding as a team of the educational problems of the country, particu-larly in the field of literacy education in its most global sense— about which I have been so insistent in this essay. We would prepare teaching materials in Geneva, as requested, with the understanding that they would be tested before they were put into general use. We would also give our opinion about other materials prepared in Bissau that might be sent to us for our evaluation.

In this manner, the project was born on which we are working jointly today: on the one side, the Commission on Education of Guinea-Bissau; on the other, the Commission on the Churches' Participation in Development which finances it, the Institute for Cultural Action and the Department of Education of the World Council of Churches. The first year has been a common learn-ing process that has enriched all of us.

# Part Two

This introduction would be even more incomplete than it now is if I did not describe some of the principal activities that have taken place since September 1975.

## *The Educational System of Guinea-Bissau*

The first of my comments is about the changes that have taken place or are going to be introduced into the educational system of the country. These modifications are in addition to those to which I referred earlier. Mario Cabral, faithful to the objectives of the Party and the orientation of the government, is preparing, through them, for the radical transformation of the system inherited from the colonizers.

I start with these changes because they will necessarily have repercussion on the education of adults—which, as I observed earlier, cannot be separated from the whole educational plan contained in the regular system of education of the country.

Conflict between an effort in the sector of informal education for adults and the educational system of a given society comes about when that effort, antagonistic to the overall social system, is the instrument that a movement or a revolutionary party seeks to use in the tactical organization of the dominated classes in order to achieve power. In the case of Guinea-Bissau, which is quite different, the important thing is the harmony between what is intended with the education of adults and what is being sought through the regular system of education in the country.

The first source of information about the changes that are taking place is Commissioner Mario Cabral. In our working meetings in Bissau, he spoke with increasing clarity about the way in which he and his associates were confronting the transformation of education in the country. I shall also refer to an interview that Cabral gave to *Nô Pintcha,* one of the newspapers in Bissau, and from which I shall quote several passages.

The new system will be constituted dialogically in relation to the infrastructure of society. The changes being introduced are never mechanical. They are part of a larger process.

Completely coherent with this vision is the concern for replacing the concept and practice that sees each part of the system as a separate entity. When each segment of the system is isolated from the others, the learner's own development is forgotten and each stage becomes an alienating and alienated moment, merely a preparation for the next stage.

The plan in which the Commission on Education of Guinea-Bissau is engaged is realistic, consonant with the country's situation. The plan recognizes the relation between the different educational levels, but it is planned so that, in each one, a particular learning task will be realized as fully as possible. Thus the relationship between Basic Instruction and the General Equivalency Course or the Middle-Level Technical School does not reduce Basic Instruction to a corridor through which a few pass with the objective of reaching the next course which, in its turn, leads only to the "elite landscape" of the university.

"Our instruction," says Mario Cabral, "will be divided into three levels: (1) Basic Instruction, with six years broken into two cycles, one of four years and the other of two; (2) General Equivalency, of three years; and (3) Middle-Level Polytechnical, which varies according to the specific requirements of the material and will be from two to three years."

Basic Instruction will become universal as soon as the Party and the State are able to bring this about. Fundamental background necessary for the full participation of any citizen in the development of the new society will be included in Basic Instruction.

We are not talking about instruction in a school that simply prepares the learners for another school, but about a real education where the content is in a constant dialectical relation with the needs of the country. In this kind of education, knowledge, resulting in practical action, itself grows out of the unity between theory and practice. For this reason, it is not possible to divorce the process of learning from its own source within the lives of the learners themselves.

The values that this education seeks are empty if they are not incarnated in life. They are only incarnated if they are put into practice. Thus, from the earliest cycle of instruction, the first four grades, participation in common experiences stimulates social solidarity rather than individualism. The principle of mutual help, practical creativity in the face of actual problems, and the unity of mental and manual labor are experienced daily. The learners begin creating new forms of behavior in accordance with the responsibility they must take within the community.

The second cycle of Basic Education, the fifth and sixth grades, involves the learners at a deeper level of the same act of learning that they experienced earlier: working and searching together not only to extend the areas of their knowledge but also to probe them more deeply. In the process, they, together with their teachers, assume the role of Subjects of their own learning.

An education that envisages making concrete such values as solidarity, social responsibility, creativity, discipline in the service of the common good, vigilance and a critical spirit—values by which PAIGC has been forged through the whole liberation process—would not be possible if, in that education, the learners continued to be what they were in the colonial educational system, mere recipients of packaged knowledge, transferred to them by their teachers. This latter process reduces them to mere "incidents" of the "educational" action of the educators.

To be identified with the reality of the country also requires that education be centered in rural reality.

"We know," says Mario Cabral, "that 90 percent of our population, at the very least, are peasants. The instruction that we are organizing must take this fact into consideration and will be, therefore, directed toward the countryside. The learner, through this education, must be able to participate as a Subject, in the necessary transformation in the local community," Cabral emphasized.

Later, referring to the necessity for extending the areas of knowledge in the second cycle of Basic Education, Mario Cabral continued, "We can say that, beginning now, we are going to introduce at this level basic notions of physics, chemistry and biology as the basis for understanding the processes of nature." Later he referred to the study of history as indispensable to the formation of militants, saying that it would be part of a basic social-science course.

"Within the courses that we are going to introduce at this

level, including geography, and with the orientation that will be given for these studies, any students who finish the course will have the kind of knowledge they need to be farmers, mechanics or progressive medical workers."

At the second level, that of General Equivalency Instruction, the goal of preparing students to respond to the most pressing needs of the country will still allow us to offer them options within the various sectors. Their scientific formation will be intensified, parallel with their general, integrated training. Militant action and social responsibility as part of a permanent process of critical reflection are, of course, indispensable. "But, above all," said the Commissioner, "practical activities will follow the characteristics and needs of each region. And we cannot leave out general skills in carpentry, electricity and agriculture that the learners will acquire through practice."

The plan also calls for the establishment of professional schools where specialization will never be distorted to become "specialism." Schools for the training of primary-school teachers, nurses' helpers, agronomists, carpenters and metal workers will be created in accord with the needs of the country. These schools will have strong ties not only to the Commission on Education but also to the other Commissions that have interest in the skills being developed.

The training offered in the General Equivalency Level schools will be continued, deepened and diversified in the Middle-Level Polytechnical Institutes. Their principal objective will be to train technicians in different fields with sufficient background to make their contribution indispensable to the transformation of the country. That training will be broad enough to avoid turning them into technocrats with such narrow, focused vision of their specialty that they are alienated from everything else.

Among the Institutes desired at this level are those dedicated to professional development, pedagogy (to prepare teachers for primary and secondary schools); nursing and the social sciences. The creation of an institute for administration as well as one for agricultural sciences is also being considered.

In all of these Institutes, young persons will be trained who, in relation to the real needs of the country, would be able to enter universities abroad. Many, of course, will be needed for continued direct engagement in national reconstruction.

In any case, to go from one of these Institutes directly into a foreign university means that certain requirements must be fulfilled. Commissioner Mario Cabral has also affirmed that only those who are most competent in their work, most committed and capable, will be chosen for courses outside the country.

There will inevitably also be criteria governing the passing of students from one level of instruction to another—from Basic Instruction to General Equivalency to Middle Polytechnical. Students will pass from one to the other "in accordance with the qualities revealed in the earlier level." Proof of seriousness in their studies, scientific and technical qualifications at the level completed, as well as indication of their moral qualities and social initiative will be considered.

One of the most important aspects of the plan, as I remarked earlier, is that it does not reduce the educational system to a funnel between the different levels of instruction. One level is not simply "preparation" for the other. Thus, students who do not go beyond Basic Instruction and who have no opportunity to broaden their knowledge in some systematic way will not have been deprived of the chance to take part in a fundamental formative experience that will enable them to contribute to the reconstruction of the country as conscious militants.

To put all this into practice requires the preparation of teachers capable of multiplying themselves through the training of others. Mario Cabral has emphasized this and gone on to say, "We will not be able to do anything in the development of different sectors of national reconstruction if we do not have sufficient teachers, both in quantity and quality. We already have funds for the creation of an Institute with this objective. We are thinking of locating it in the center of the country, perhaps at Mansabá."

The intention of the Commission is to graduate, initially, 250 lead-teachers who, after a year's experience in the field, will participate in a seminar for continuing education, based on the evaluation of their own experience. The Institute will prepare teachers for the different levels of instruction. Admission to the courses will depend on different criteria depending on the level at which the candidate intends to teach. Thus, those who want to teach in Basic Instruction will have to have completed six years. The duration of their course will be three years. Those aspiring to teach in the second level of Basic Instruction must have completed nine years and will undergo three years' additional training.

To teach in the General Equivalency level, students will have to have completed 11 years. Their course will also be three years.

"We can say," affirms Mario Cabral, "that this Institute will be, in embryonic form, the first university of the country. For those who intend to become professors in a teacher-training school, 11 years of schooling will be required, and they will have a four-year training course at the Institute of Pedagogy."

And now I shall speak in a kind of parenthesis: I believe that I will not be betraying the spirit of the Commission on Education in Guinea-Bissau when I affirm the importance it is giving to the gradual scientific formation of their students. This will result in increasing understanding of reality as the students act on that reality. It has nothing to do with "scientism," which mythologizes science and distorts reason. In the same way, as they come to recognize the necessary relation between education and production, they will not fall into the error of glorifying production and, with it, consumerism.

One of the basic aspects of the Guinean system that is being created, it seems to me, is the invitation being offered to students to develop solidarity and social responsibility through their practice of service. They come to see work as the source of knowledge and, in the production of what is socially necessary, they discover an authentic camaraderie instead of the competition engendered by individualism. This is in addition to their necessary scientific formation.

"The real objective of the new system," says Mario Cabral emphatically, "is to eliminate the remains of the colonial system in order to contribute to the objectives of PAIGC to create new persons, workers aware of their historical responsibilities and of avenues of creative, effective participation in the process of social transformation. We hope to make this desire real through the ever-growing understanding of the concrete necessities of the country, through the definition of our plan for development, and through the work itself, realized at the level of the schools as well as through discussions in all the collective organizations. These discussions would include not only the technical aspects but also the needs of life itself."

Later, however, he warns, "The whole plan for the transformation of the national instructional system will not be worth anything if there are not similar transformations in all of the other sectors of activity.

"It is possible," said Mario Cabral in the last meeting we had with him in Bissau in September of 1976, "that, in a certain sense, education initiates the challenge. It is necessary, moreover, that structural transformations be made, giving support to the challenge, so that the practice implied in the challenge may become concrete."

Following the normal practice of Guinea-Bissau—that of open discussions always encouraged by PAIGC and the Government—Commissioner Mario Cabral held a great public meeting that brought together students and their families, professors, educational functionaries and other interested persons. He assessed the activities in the year that had just ended, and spoke of the Commission's principal tasks for the next school year, designated as the Second Year of Organization (*Nô Pintcha*, November 1976).

The first part of his address focused clearly and directly on the difficulties that they had confronted, beginning in October 1974 when PAIGC, entering Bissau, took over the government of the whole country. He spoke of the mass withdrawal of secondary-school teachers. Most of them were "members of the military, here to oppress our people and to put obstacles in the way of our progress." He noted the lack of experienced leadership in the Commission on Education in regard to the tasks of planning, organizing and reorganizing the curriculum and the uncertainty about what to do in the face of the educational inheritance from colonial times. It was clear that it would be impossible to make changes from one day to the next. The Commissioner told us that it was at this time that the idea of the systematic closing of all the schools was suggested and discarded. "Some wanted us to close our schools in order to reorganize the Commission and be able to have the kind of instruction and the means of education that we, in fact, needed. This was only a dream. If we had done that, we would still not be ready to begin our classes today because we have not even yet achieved the perfect conditions required by such ideal forms of instruction."

He then referred to certain positive achievements and to some of the mistakes made, the dedication of some, and the failures of others. Highlighting what happened between September 1974 and September 1975 as a learning period for everyone dedicated to the educational task, he called this period the "Year of Experimentation" from which emerged the need to constitute the following year as the "First Year of Organization."

In analyzing the accomplishments of the year just ended, the First Year of Organization, and criticizing again the failures that should never be hidden, he stressed the accomplishments and the strong spirit of the majority of the comrades in the Commission on Education; he spoke of the effort expended in the structuring of the Commission. He told of the results obtained through this structure, with the creation, for example, of bodies such as the Policy Council, the Technical Teaching Council, and the Administrative Council, all of them bodies that function in a dynamic manner, facilitating constant discussions regarding the educational reality in the country.

The importance of these Councils is, obviously, not in their mere existence, since they also exist within other ministries of education. The important thing is the practice that has evolved, coherent with the objectives that they serve, and the climate of search and dialogue that characterizes them. "Their activity is, in fact, what allows us to advance in our work," said Cabral.

Later in his address as he spoke of the praxis about which he is constantly thinking, Cabral said that one of his principal preoccupations was the relation between the school at whatever level and the local, regional and national reality. "One of our principal objectives is to make the connection between the school and life—to relate it to the community in which it exists, to the small village or to the neighborhood. We strive, as well, to link the school to productive labor in the area and, especially, to agriculture; to bring it closer to the mass organizations, to JACC, to the Young Pioneers, the labor unions, and the women's organizations. Much of this task has already been achieved and, in some regions, extremely efficiently. In the Bafatá region, for example, of 106 schools, 96 are producing from their fields. In Bissau, even though we have not achieved the same results, a lot has happened also.

"It has been," continued Mario Cabral, "in the school at Có that we have achieved the maximum linkage between the school and productive work and between the school and the local population, with the integration of the people in the area in the cultural activities of the school. We can consider the school at Có as the best in the whole country during the year that has just ended."

Elza and I feel a particular closeness to this school at Có—the Maxim Gorki Center for the Formation of Teachers. It has assumed great importance not only in the educational efforts of the whole country but has made particular contributions to the development of models for adult literacy education. We have visited it on each of our trips to Guinea-Bissau and we are always deeply impressed by the dedication of the teachers, whose critical optimism penetrates everything they do to carry out their tasks.

The Commissioner's report highlighted the following achievements of the academic year 1975–76: (1) the participation of middle-school students from Bissau in productive activities; (2) the creation of a Party committee to work with primary-school teachers, both in their cultural work and in the social and political activities that support it; (3) the exceptional contributions of children and their teachers in celebrating the twentieth anniversary of PAIGC, especially their gymnastic exhibition; (4) the seminars in which those responsible for education in various parts of the country came together to discuss their experience, exchanging ideas about the overcoming of difficulties; and (5) efforts to promote the continuing education of teachers and the participation of some in the training and retraining of others.

"This year," continued Mario Cabral, "we were able to complete the training of 30 primary-school teachers—a number equalling the total that the Portuguese colonialists trained in 500 years of domination."

This last statistic speaks eloquently for the excellence of the colonial system.

Mario Cabral dedicated the last part of his assessment to the principal tasks of the Commission on Education for the academic year 1976–77, the Second Year of Organization. He mentioned three major tasks, the first being the contribution of the schools of the country to the Third Party Congress. "Comrades, what will be our contribution to this Congress?" he asked.

In the reply that the Commisioner made to his own question, he neither suggests nor requires the usual ritual participation of students in such empty efforts as memorizing the history of PAIGC nor the writing of "made-to-order" compositions about the Party and its history. A good Party militant himself, he knows its principles because he has been part of the long process of their development. The Commissioner is well aware that ritual activities are not the way to motivate teachers and students to make a real contribution to the Congress. He also refrains from manipulative suggestions about mass affiliations with the Party since he knows that what is required is both awareness and dedication to the cause of the working people rather than new, opportunistic members for the Party.

Therefore he makes an appeal to the students and teachers that they work together as hard as they can to obtain more positive results than those already achieved. Such conscious participation in the effort would be a distinctive contribution to the Year of the Third Congress.

"The second task to which we shall dedicate ourselves is that of organizing a campaign of adult literacy," says the Commissioner, commenting on what has already been done and on what must be expanded and deepened in the year to come. He refers to the work accomplished in the various regions by means of "brigades" trained and supervised by the Coordinating Commission on Literacy.

"This year we went out into the regions. Next year we need far greater participation of our students, not only from Bissau but from all areas of the country."

As part of the second task, the government, through the Commission on Education, will sponsor the first international seminar to be held in Bissau. This will be coordinated by the Ministers of Education of Guinea-Bissau and the Cape Verde Islands, Saõ Tomé e Principe, Angola and Mozambique. Delegations from these countries will come together to evaluate the praxis in their own countries in the field of education with special concern for adult literacy education.

The results of such a meeting should provide an opportunity for rich learning on the part of participants and also a practical impetus for collaboration among them despite the uniqueness of each country. The same basic struggle for national reconstruction engages all.

The third task emphasizes the relation between the school and productive work, attempting on the one hand to improve these relations and, on the other, to extend them, as far as possible, throughout the nation.

"Comrade Amilcar Cabral used to say, 'I am a simple African who wishes only to pay his debt to his own people and to live to the full his own epoch.' May we all pay our debts to our people and live fully our own time. Our historical epoch demands total liberation, total independence, and our total engagement in overcoming illiteracy and combating underdevelopment in national reconstruction," concluded Mario Cabral.

I do not know whether, without afflicting my readers too much, I have accomplished what I intended in this introduction. From the beginning, I have wanted to offer a picture—that could never, of course, be complete—of what is happening in Guinea-Bissau. All of the achievements have interested us intensely; from them we have learned a great deal. Our effort has often taken the form of active involvement rather than a narrowly professional contribution.

The richness of the Guinean experience has been such that it has been impossible to speak of it in a few words. And thus I must still prolong my observations in spite of necessary omissions regarding certain details that I know to be of great importance.

## The Maxim Gorki Center at Có

We visited the Maxim Gorki Training Center for the first time in February 1976. Elza and I went with the team from IDAC, with Mario Cabral himself as our guide.

Early in the morning on our way to Có, a tiny rural settlement near Cacheu, about fifty kilometers north of Bissau, Mario Cabral spoke with enthusiasm of the Center and told us something of its history.

In November 1975 a group of educators had sought out the Commissioner. Without any preliminaries, they laid before him their plan to create a training center for teachers in an old military installation vacated by the colonial army at the time of independence. The installation was like so many others that the colonial army had spread throughout the countryside, surrounded by barbed wire and mines. Like the others, this one had been a fortification for the invaders and had also served as a site where they tortured nationals, sometimes to the point of death. On many occasions the Portuguese themselves, terrified by the strong determination of their prisoners, had increasingly become imprisoned within their own camps.

Much needed to be done to clean and improve the installation. In a strange way, without wanting to, the Portuguese had made this a natural location for a future political-pedagogical training center. Just as the people had seen those who were tortured as heroes, they were ready to see the educators who came to transform the barracks as new heroes, inheritors of the earlier ones. I visited an early hero's grave that had recently been identified by the people of the community. He and his comrades had paid a price for their rebellion and their desire to stand on the side of their own people.

At the time of our visit, four months had passed since the

group of educators had begun the process of installing the center. Reflecting their vivid experiences in education in the liberated zones, they had dedicated themselves completely to cleaning the barracks, razing unnecessary small buildings, improving sanitary conditions, planting trees, and restoring the well that now furnishes excellent water. With equal dedication they had begun to plan for the administration of the center and its effective integration into the life of the surrounding community. They designed the political-pedagogical activities to be undertaken and prepared to receive the first group of students.

Just as those who fought side by side with Amilcar Cabral understood that their dream must be incarnated in the people in order to become a reality, in the same way, the educators at Có involved the neighboring populations in the development of their dream for a training center. They interpreted the project and mobilized the population around both the idea and the necessary practical activities. People came from all around to clear the land, bringing their own work tools. The team and the local people worked side by side. The growing dialogue between them was sealed in their mutual activity on behalf of the center.

With each day that passes, the center resembles more closely a people's university, born at the heart of the life of working people, based on their productive labor, and dedicated to systematizing knowledge resulting from practical experience. The Center at Có is seeking to overcome the dichotomies that exist between mental and manual labor and between learning and teaching.

The activities of the very first class of students have also been in accord with this principle. They have devoted themselves to productive labor, closely associated with their intellectual work. The patterns established in the liberated zones have been faithfully adapted and expanded at Có. Last September I saw their cultivated fields—wheat, corn, potatoes, fruit, vegetables. In cooperation with the Ministry on Agriculture, they have also begun to raise chickens, ducks, pigs and sheep. Through these efforts, the center is becoming self-sufficient.

The participation of the students in productive work is highly positive in itself. It would be unfortunate if they did not also have sources of knowledge more diverse than those offered by agricultural activities. It would be equally unfortunate if the training and retraining of basic instruction teachers were divorced from practical educational activities. If the students simply went from their practical activities of planting and harvesting into classrooms for traditional lectures about how to teach, their training would be defective. While the school does not have its own primary school, an arrangement has been made with a school in the neighborhood for the students to carry out practical teaching activities.

Even though they must contend with enormous obstacles of a material nature that need not be enumerated here, the Center attempts to base training on the analysis of practice. In the very practice of analyzing practice, the unity between the act of teaching and the act of learning is being experienced by the students. This unity is actually being lived not only in the activities between teachers and students at the Center but also between the teachers and students as a team and the people who live around the Center, with whom they have a growing relationship.

In the dialectical unity between teaching and learning, the saying "Whoever knows, teaches the one who doesn't" takes on a revolutionary meaning. When the one who knows understands first that the process by which he learned is social and, second, that in teaching something to another he is also learning something that he did not know already, then both are changed. This is the spirit one feels at Có. The same spirit characterized PAIGC and the political-pedagogical training center at Conakry that grew out of the living example of Amilcar Cabral. The same spirit gives life to the continuation of the struggle and to education in the liberated zones. The school at Có is part of the same continuity.

The strength of the communication between the people and the Center has made possible one of the best examples of literacy education for adults in Guinea-Bissau. It was initiated in June 1976 and we visited it in September.

Directed by members of the Coordinating Commission for

Literacy Education of Adults, this experiment was actually carried out by students resident at Có for training. It has produced a remarkable socio-economic, cultural census—the best done in any area of the country. On the basis of the census, appropriate generative words were chosen and a dynamic approach to literacy education began.

Little by little the Center extended and intensified its activities. "We have done our best," said the Director, Jorge Ampa, "to fulfill the objective of our school in relating it to the life of the population. A team of three students trained in first aid operate a clinic. It is open daily and has sometimes attended more than 100 persons in a month. Between April and July of this year 294 were treated."

Preventive medicine has a high priority. The Center has sponsored with the local committee a series of meetings to discuss certain popular beliefs regarding health care and to analyze aspects of "magic" in those beliefs—the "weaknesses of culture" referred to by Amilcar Cabral.

These meetings are really seminars on health problems. They are held in clearings under the shade of a tree or under woven straw shelters constructed by the people. They focus on social practice in the community and serve to increase the people's comprehension of the world around them just as PAIGC has so characteristically done. In the final analysis, to overcome the "weaknesses of culture" as these are found in social practice, the practices themselves must be completely transformed. And this, of course, requires social change in relation to production. Since the change cannot be mechanical but, rather, dialectical, political-pedagogical activity is necessary. Health education seminars are, therefore, tied not only to an analysis of health but to a critical understanding of overall goals for national reconstruction. Health is seen in relation to production and to the social implications of any given mode of production. The discussions in the seminars often become political debates.

Whatever activity gives rise to political consciousness raising —whether it be health education, means of production, or adult literacy efforts—there is a basic unity of approach. The Director stressed that all of the activities are planned and carried out in cooperation with the local committee in every village.

It is my conviction that the permanent teaching staff of the Center needs to consider the basic relations between health, education and the means of production in ongoing seminars in addition to their more specific interests in discrete fields. The relationship underlies everything they do with the students who come to the Center to study. Amilcar Cabral was referring to the significance of the underlying relationship when he said, "The means of production represents at every stage in history the result of incessant search for a dynamic equilibrium between the forces of production and the political system governing the social utilization of these forces."[8] Seminars on cultural aliena-tion induced in certain sectors of the population by the pres-ence of the colonial forces would also be extremely useful to the teaching staff.

The first class at Có had 30 students; the second 60. In 1977–78 they will be able to take 100 students. To the degree that they are able to intensify their political-pedagogical work with the population of the villages, their understanding of the reality that conditions village life will become increasingly clear.

As the teams are involved more and more deeply in a process of mutual learning, they will discover that, on the one hand, they are the Subjects of that learning and, on the other hand, that the popular groups with whom they enter into dialogue are themselves the Subjects. Learning from and with these groups, the teams from the Center have a task from which they cannot escape and for which they must be well prepared: that of help-ing, in the authentic sense of this word, the groups to analyze their praxis and to systematize their learning derived from this praxis. Thus they go beyond mere opinion about the facts to the critical comprehension of those same facts.

It is on the basis of such a task that the Center is becoming a true university of the people. Both the teams and the groups take their own daily lives as the object of their reflection in a process of this nature. They are required to stand at a distance from the daily lives in which they are generally immersed and to which they often attribute an aura of permanence. Only at a distance can they get a perspective that permits them to emerge from that daily routine and begin their own independent development. The necessary precondition to taking a distance from "dailiness" is the analysis of past and present practice and the extension of this analysis into their possible future, remembering always that every practice is social in character.

When people are able to see and analyze their own way of being in the world of their immediate daily life, including the life of their villages, and when they can perceive the rationale for the factors on which their daily life is based, they are enabled to go far beyond the narrow horizons of their own village and of the geographical area in which it is located, to gain a global perspective on reality.

Political-pedagogical activity such as this—one that puts a dialectical theory of knowledge in practice—becomes, in itself, a fundamental dimension of the task of national reconstruction. Out of such an understanding of national reconstruction, a new society can evolve and a new type of intellectual emerge. The unity between manual and intellectual work and between practice and theory becomes real.

I am absolutely convinced that if the school at Có continues its practice of organizing with the people the systematic knowledge derived from their own daily experience, it can contribute to the formation of the new intellectual and become the university center of which I spoke earlier. Activity in response both to the growing curiosity of the people and to local, regional and national needs perceived by them will make it possible for the school to develop community nurses, agricultural specialists, mechanics, electricians and persons knowledgable in raising poultry. Ongoing evaluation of practice will increase the skills and overall ability of the people in specific fields.

These future specialists will be educated in a school that is as broad as life itself and will develop a critical comprehension— neither narrow nor ingenuous—regarding their own praxis within the larger praxis of the society in which they participate. Both the specific and the social practice of this critical comprehension demand a political formation as thorough as their technical and professional training.

In the face of everything this school stands for, it would be a contradiction if the administration were controlled entirely by its director. In fact the director, the permanent teaching staff, and the teachers who come there to study participate equally in the school's governance. Each week the governing body meets to make an evaluation of what has occurred in the past week. In an unpressured atmosphere, they discuss ideas and problems. As far as possible they avoid the necessity of taking a vote. "When we vote," says Jorge Ampa, "it is because there is disagreement."

In these meetings of the governing body, general directions for the life of the Center are outlined and carefully considered. All plans for activities in the community are discussed. These matters are again debated in an assembly that includes all of the students. It is not rare for new ideas and proposals that enrich the thinking done by the governing body and benefit the whole community to come out of these assemblies.

It would be similarly contradictory if this school, linked as it is to the Commission on Education—50 kilometers away and with very difficult conditions for communication—depended upon that central body for the solution of its routine problems and for the development and implementation of its work plans. The only requirement placed upon the school is that its plans be in harmony with the objectives for education in the nation. In the final analysis, the Commission on Education operates at a national level as the school at Có operates at its level, openly and democratically. Instead of asphyxiating initiative with bureaucratic requirements, the Commission stimulates and even requires initiative and creativity, without allowing its action to get lost in a world of papers coming and going, filling a vacuum with bureaucratic uselessness. There are no inoperative vacant spots "filled" with people, either in the Commission on Education or in the school at Có. The latter has become an example of creativity and activism modelled after the experimental work of PAIGC in the liberated zones.

"Within the Second Year of Organization," says its director, "we will work harder and better, concentrating our action on the Third Party Congress that will be meeting very soon. We intend to celebrate the event by intensifying our practical and theoretical activities at the Center. If we received 100 percent approval in this past year, we are going to do our best to achieve the same result in the year to come."

It was not without reason that the Maxim Gorki Center for Teacher Training in the town of Có was considered the model school for the whole country during the academic year 1975–76.

## A Visit to a Rural Area

In February 1976, in a place a few kilometers to the north of Có, I attended a meeting between a significant group of peasants of the community and the Commissioner on Education. Political leaders of the area were also present.

In the process of our learning about the reality of Guinea-Bissau, this was the first time that we had come in contact with a group of peasants. It was intensely interesting to us, obviously, to discover how they saw themselves in relation to the Party and the government and in the general picture of national reconstruction. What did this struggle mean to them as a continuation of that other struggle for national liberation? It had been a struggle to which they had given their full support—as far as they could in the face of the colonialist repression to which they had been forced to submit.

The meeting did not take place in a formal hall but in the shade of an enormous and very ancient tree. The people demonstrated their hospitality by receiving the delegation in the inviting shade of that tree, in intimate relation with their own natural world.

My impression was that the shaded area beneath that tree was a kind of political-cultural center—a place for informal conversation—where they made their work plans together. I also thought how such a place, taking advantage of the shade, might be used for programs of nonformal education.

As I went toward the tree, admiring its thick foliage, I remembered that it had been in the shade of just such trees that Amilcar Cabral met with armed militants during the struggle to evaluate their action against the colonialist armies. At such times, military and tactical analyses never failed to be accompanied by political discussions and debates about culture. Through this means the permanent leadership squadrons were formed.

I remembered also other things that a militant had said to me about the many meetings that Amilcar Cabral had had with peasants. Cabral, while directing some research regarding agrarian reality in Guinea-Bissau, had traveled throughout the country. He took advantage of the opportunity to talk discreetly with those whom he met about the oppressive reality in which the people found themselves. In these conversations he was able to identify future leaders for PAIGC. Three years after the initiation of the census, on September 19, 1956, PAIGC was founded.*

Once, during a conversation with peasants in the shade of a tree, Cabral arose, holding the seed of a dende palm in his hand. He chose a good place, dug a hole and planted the seed. Afterwards, looking at the peasants gathered about him, he said, "We, the people of Guinea-Bissau, will accomplish many things before the palm tree that grows from this seed will bear fruit."

"Years later," the young man told me, "there was a meeting of the committee of PAIGC in that region beside the palm tree that had just borne its first fruit."

In making that speech Cabral spoke a language of hope. He did not confine himself to the spoken word but dramatized the idea by planting the seed. This was not the false hope of one who hopes for the sake of hoping and lives on the basis of vain hope. Hope is true and well founded only when it grows out of the unity between action that transforms the world and critical reflection regarding the meaning of that action.

As he spoke that language of hope with the peasants, Cabral began putting down his own roots in the midst of the people. With the formation of PAIGC, the process of re-Africanization associated with "class suicide," so necessary for African intellectuals, was intensified.

---

*This census was determined by the then Ministry for Overseas Affairs of Portugal. It was carried out in 1953 to fulfill the obligation of the Portuguese delegation to an FAO (Food and Agricultural Organization conference of the United Nations in 1947 when, through the delegates, Portugal had agreed to carry out an agricultural census of all of its overseas possessions.

As our own meeting in the shade of the tree began, Mario Cabral, in very few words, explained our presence in Guinea-Bissau and the work that we were carrying on together with national leaders in the field of education. He ended by saying that he was there as the person ultimately responsible for education in the country, to hear and to talk with them freely about their most pressing needs.

Immediately, then, the five oldest members of the group gathered together in a small circle within the larger circle, talking among themselves in low voices, while all the rest remained silent. A Western educator, insensitive to other cultures and convinced of the efficacy of his own ways, would probably see in all of this signs of inefficiency, as though they had not "made serious plans for this meeting."

A youth near me said, "They are talking among themselves in order to establish the order in which they will speak, as well as to define the points about which they will speak. This is their custom."

At a given point the five began to speak, one by one. They were exceedingly rich in their use of metaphors and gestures, with which they underlined their affirmations and their meanings.

Referring to the violence of the colonialists, one of them bowed low and bowed again, curving his body, living the word with which he described the terrible treatment received. He walked from one side to the other within the circle of the shade in which we stood, using the movements of his body to express some aspect of the story he told. None of them spoke ecstatically, disassociating his body from the words he spoke. None spoke only to be heard. In Africa the word is also to be seen, part of the necessary gesture. No one in Africa, with the exception of the de-Africanized intellectuals, denies his roots, or reveals fear or shame in using his body to express his meaning.

And while we saw and heard them speaking, with the force of their metaphors and the easy movements of their bodies, we thought of the innumerable possibilities that were opened for a liberating education by these wellsprings of African culture.

They spoke also of the present moment, of their desire to participate in the struggle for national reconstruction. They spoke, at the same time, of the difficulties that they confronted.

The oldest among them, the one who spoke last in the shade of that enormous tree, spoke to all of us in the language of hope.

"The PAIGC," he said, "for all of its 20 years, is still a child. Twenty years are many in the life of a person, but not in the life of a people, or of a Party. The good thing about PAIGC is that it has learned to walk with the people. I will not see the great things that the people of Guinea-Bissau, PAIGC and the government will do. But the children of our children will see these things. For this very reason, it is necessary that I who will not see that time, and all of us, do now what is necessary for our time."

Every time we come to Guinea-Bissau, we reserve time not only for reencounters and return visits but for new encounters and new visits. These make us more and more aware, in a very intimate way, of reality. New encounters and visits are absolutely fundamental to our praxis with the national teams. They are part of the method of work that we adopted and through which we attempt to see and hear, to question and discuss. In these visits and encounters, we are always attentive to the smallest detail that attracts our attention and challenges our curiosity to some new reflection with our national colleagues.

In our trips to the country we could not participate efficiently in the evaluation seminars with the Coordinating Commission on Literacy if (1) we remained only in Bissau and did not observe the practice in other areas of the country, or (2) we did not try to understand what was going on in other sectors of activity aside from adult literacy education.

## Activities in Adult Literacy Education in 1975–76

In the following considerations with which I will conclude this introduction, I shall attempt a synthesis of the activities that have taken place recently in the field of adult literacy education in Guinea-Bissau.

There is one point that it seems to me necessary to underline above all others. That is the "mass line" that characterizes the literacy work in the country. What is intended, fundamentally, is to see the literacy education of adults as a political act, coherent with the principles of PAIGC. It is an act that informs the action of the government and is based on a real involvement of the people. Wherever programs of adult literacy are initiated, in accordance with the priorities established by the Party and the government, they are taken over, as far as possible, by the local population. In this way, an indispensable relation is established between the adult literacy programs and the political committees of the villages or city neighborhoods. Through these committees, the educators and local teachers, themselves activists, are put directly in touch with the people. What really characterizes the "mass line" and defines it as such is its revolutionary anti-elitism, its anti-paternalism, and the way in which local people assume the role of Subjects through their participation in programing the campaign. A dynamic relation between tactics and strategy is maintained. The strategy is to integrate the campaign into the overall plan for the society. The tactics are to initiate the campaign only in areas where conditions are already favorable for such activity. To say the campaign is national does not mean that it must begin everywhere at once. If conditions are right or are at least partially favorable, the efforts toward literacy move more rapidly. Something concrete results. If the conditions do not exist or are very far from being favorable, literacy efforts have no meaning. For this reason, there is no way to confuse the "mass line" with the voluntarist approach to literacy that depends on generalized planning rather than on careful tactics consistent with local reality.

A literacy campaign that follows the "mass line" will sooner or later be generalized to include the whole society. Although this is true, it does not necessarily follow that every literacy campaign that is aimed at the whole of the society is part of the "mass line." The establishment of priority zones in Guinea-Bissau for the launching of the literacy campaign is not a negation of the "mass line" but a means of realizing it.

In contrast with what happens in the usual voluntarist literacy campaign, the "mass line" demands of those involved that they live in permanent tension between patience and impatience. Voluntarist literacy campaigns, on the contrary, result in the negation of the tension, leaving those involved in a constant state of impatience. In order to break the tension, they tend to accelerate the process whether or not conditions are right. This results in teaching without learning and the "transfer" of knowledge because "there is no time to lose."

Breaking the tension between patience and impatience, under such circumstances, inevitably leads to teaching without dialogue. No matter what the intention, knowledge is presented as something finished, already concluded. There is often an unperceived contradiction between one's perception of the learning process and one's practice. The impatient educator often transfers knowledge like a package while discoursing volubly on the dynamic nature of knowledge.

When there is a rupture in the tension between patience and impatience, the opposite situation might also exist: impatience might almost disappear. In this case educators may fall into passivity. "Let everything stay as it is so that we can see what will happen" is an attitude that has nothing in common with the militantly revolutionary "mass line." Patience is not conformity. The best way to accomplish those things that are impossible today is to do today whatever *is* possible.

Amilcar Cabral kept this tension. In his revolutionary praxis and in his reflections on it that he left us in his writings, the tension was always apparent: "We must walk rapidly but not run," he said. "We must not be opportunists, nor allow our enthusiasms to make us lose the vision of concrete reality. It is more important to begin an armed struggle with apparent delays but with the guarantee of continuity than to begin too early or in any moment when we do not have conditions that guarantee continuity and victory for our people." And, later, he goes on, "To know our strengths means to have at every instant complete consciousness of what we are able to do. It means also to evaluate our possibilities in every area, in every unit of the armed forces, to act always in accord with these possibilities and to do our best to increase our strength and our capability, in both men and material. It means never to do less than we can or ought to do, but not to pretend, ever, to do things that we are really not ready to do."[9]

It is on the basis of these principles, valid not only for the liberation struggle yesterday but for national reconstruction today, that the government of Guinea-Bissau, through its Commission on Education, is working in the field of adult literacy education. And it is for this reason that, as I stressed earlier, although the campaign is national in scope, it is beginning in those areas that make a valid experience possible, offering those who participate the rich, dynamic opportunities for learning on which they can build in the future.

This aspect of the preparation of cadres able to put into practice a pedagogy that coincides with these basic principles cannot help becoming a fundamental factor in the general picture of a literacy campaign such as the one in which the government of Guinea-Bissau is now engaged. The necessary competence results from a unity of practice and theory. It does not come from "training" in a certain number of technical skills, as is the case in the advanced capitalist societies where more and more training in a limited number of skills takes place.[10]

This aspect of the program is the direct responsibility of the Coordinating Commission for Adult Literacy* working in close cooperation with the Commissioner Mario Cabral.

None of the activities of the Coordinating Commission is easy to carry out, nor do the results always correspond with the hopes placed in them. The mistakes that have occurred at one time or another, resulting from poor planning or lack of adequate understanding of local reality, are analyzed by the Commission—a process that, in itself, is not without difficulties. In the exercise of self-criticism, the Commission members are also learning how to overcome the problems encountered. The important thing is to be convinced once

---

*This Commission is increasingly operating as an intercommissional entity. It reports through the Commission on Education to the National Commission on Literacy in which all of the Commissioners whose responsibilities relate at all to literacy participate. The President of the Council of State himself serves as the President of the National Commission on Literacy. Their task is to outline the general policies and lines of action to be followed by the Coordinating Commission for Adult Literacy. We have participated in two meetings of this national commission and were impressed by the quality of their discussions.

again, with Amilcar Cabral, that "the errors we commit should not discourage us, just as the victories should not make us forget the mistakes."[11]

In 1975–76 the principal task of the Commission at the national level has been to foster closer working relations with the Commissions on Health, Agriculture, Internal Services and Information. They have also tried to cooperate fully with local party committees, with the mass organizations like those for youth and labor, and they have worked closely with the Center at Có. Major attention has been directed toward the training of leadership cadres. Culture Circles have been created wherever continuity could be assured, and small nucleus programs have been organized in all the priority areas. In addition to these activities, brigades organized by the Commission have traveled widely in Bissau and in other priority zones. Their task has been to interpret the role of literacy education as integral to national reconstruction. Public opinion has been mobilized.

In full recognition of the errors committed in their first year, the Commission is now preparing for participation in the Second Year of Organization within which the national literacy campaign has been designated as one of the government's three principal tasks.

In its report made during the month of May 1976 the Commission said, "We want to refer especially to the tremendous support we have received from the leaders of the Party and the State that attests to the importance being given to literacy." This support was proven many times in the contacts that preceded the sending of one of the brigades into some area of the country. The President, Luiz Cabral, the different Commissions that are part of the National Commission on Literacy, all of the Commissioners, mass organizations and state organizations have all provided valuable contacts.

During a recent visit in September 1976 to the school at Có, we included trips to four small villages in the region. We were able to observe in the Culture Circles, held in the straw-roofed shelters, the extraordinary literacy work that was in progress there, growing out of the political-pedagogical presence of the school at Có.

We also dedicated eight days of that trip to a seminar to evaluate all the work of the Commission. The evaluation, as mentioned earlier, does not consist of a process in which we take the Coordinating Commission and its work as the object of our analysis, discussing them with "professional airs." Rather, we and the Commission members together engage in dialogue about what is being done. We are active Subjects in the evaluation as we try to analyze together the cause of whatever failures there have been and to study alternative means of overcoming them.

The programs carried out in the armed forces, through FARP, revealed a high index of efficiency. It was not pure coincidence that the most positive efforts in the civilian area were those in the villages around the school at Có.

One conclusion of the evaluation seminar was that the Commission should try, as far as possible, to establish a relation (in addition to its normal linkage to the local party committee) with whatever service facility it could find locally—whether that be a health clinic, a school, a production cooperative or other service group—so that the deep communication with the people enjoyed by these activities might also become a real source of support for literacy education programs.

Of one thing we are sure: moving ahead in "patient impatience" and, therefore, with confidence, the work of adult literacy education in Guinea-Bissau is more than a promise. It is a reality.

In concluding this introduction, there are two points that must not be omitted. First, I must express deep gratitude, not only my own but that of the team from IDAC and of the Department of Education of the World Council of Churches, to the people, to PAIGC, and to the government of Guinea-Bissau, for the opportunity they have given us both to learn so much and to teach, and, in this way, to participate in the effort to reconstruct the country.

Second, in my own name and Elza's, I wish to speak of how much our involvement in Guinea-Bissau has called forth a nostalgia for Brazil—a deep longing that is both calm and "well behaved"—and for those now-distant years in Culture Circles, as lively as the ones at Có, where we learned so much from our own people.

PAULO FREIRE

*Geneva*
*Winter 1976*

# THE LETTERS
# TO GUINEA-BISSAU

*"The struggle for liberation which is the most complex expression of the cultural strength of a people, of their identity and their dignity, enriches the culture and opens new perspectives for its development. Manifestations of the culture take on new content and forms of expression. They become in this way powerful instruments of information and of political formation not only in the struggle for independence but in the larger battle for progress. . . . The dynamics of the struggle require the practice of democracy, of criticism and self-criticism, the growing participation of the people in taking charge of their own lives, literacy, the creation of schools and health services, the formation of 'cadres' who come from the midst of the peasants and workers, and many other developments which impel people to set forth upon the road of cultural progress. All of this makes it very clear that the struggle for liberation is not only a cultural fact but also a factor of culture."*

AMILCAR CABRAL

"THE ROLE OF CULTURE IN THE LIBERATION STRUGGLE,"
SPEECH DELIVERED TO A UNESCO CONFERENCE IN PARIS,
JULY 3–7, 1972

# Letter 1

Geneva
January 26, 1975

Engineer Mario Cabral
Commissioner of State for Education and Culture
Bissau, Republic of Guinea-Bissau

*Dear Comrade,*

A few days ago, I received a letter from someone connected with Guinea-Bissau who told me of his recent meeting in Bissau with you and the president of the State Council. He mentioned the possibility that a team of which I am a part might make a contribution to the government's work in adult literacy education. He also suggested that I write you right away in order to initiate a conversation about how such a contribution might be made concrete.

As a man from the Third World and as an educator completely committed to this world, I could have no other reaction —nor could my colleagues—than to offer to the people of Guinea-Bissau whatever small contribution we might make.

Since it is not possible, at the moment, for me to go to Bissau to discuss personally the basis for our participation, I am writing to ask whether you could come to Geneva for two or three days or if, perhaps, one of your assistants could do so.

In such a meeting, for which I would be free beginning the 19th of April, we could discuss not only the way in which our contribution might be made but also the general lines of adult literacy education in Guinea-Bissau. Literacy education for adults, seen in the perspective of liberation, is a creative act. It can never be reduced to a mechanical matter, in which the so-called literacy worker (teacher) deposits his/her own word in the learners, as though their conscious bodies were simply empty, waiting to be filled by that word. Such a technique is mechanical and relies on memorizing; the learners are made to repeat again and again, with their eyes closed, all together: la, le, li, lo, lu; ba, be, bi, bo, bu; ta, te, ti, to, tu, a monotonous chant which implies above all a false conception of the act of knowing. "Repeat, repeat, in order that you may learn" is one of the principles of this false understanding of the act of knowing.

From a liberation perspective, which is that of Guinea-Bissau and is ours as well, literacy education of adults is, on the contrary, a continuation of the formidable struggle which your people together with their leaders began, now long ago, to conquer THEIR WORD. From such a perspective, literacy education cannot escape from the depths of the people, from their productive activity, from their culture. It will not become hardened in the soulless cold of bureaucratized schools in which primers designed by distant intellectuals—sometimes with the best of intentions—emphasize the mechanical memorizing to which I referred before.

Literacy education of adults, as we understand it, is one dimension of cultural action for liberation. It cannot, for this reason, be thought of in isolation, but always in relation to other aspects of cultural action taken in its totality. To discuss it means to discuss also the social, economic and cultural politics of the country. As a matter of fact it was this perception of the interrelationship of all of the parts of a totality that impressed me so greatly in Amilcar Cabral, as well as his critical comprehension of the role of culture in the struggle for liberation which is, as he emphasized, "a cultural fact and also a factor of culture."

I realize how difficult it would be for you to be absent from the country even for two or three days. Nevertheless, I take the liberty of urging you to come because of what it would represent in making concrete something that both stimulates and challenges us.

*Fraternally,*
*Paulo Freire*

# Letter 2
Geneva
April 1975

Engineer Mario Cabral
Commissioner of State for Education and Culture
Bissau, Republic of Guinea-Bissau

*Dear Comrade Mario Cabral,*

I have just received your letter confirming the interest of your government in our collaboration.

I do not believe it is necessary for me to tell you with what satisfaction the team of the Institute for Cultural Action (IDAC), of which I am a part, and the Department of Education of the World Council of Churches (WCC), where I work, received this news.

I have already expressed in my first letter the desire of all of us to work with you and to make our contribution, no matter how small, to the search in which you find yourselves involved for both a new practice and a new vision of education responsive to the objectives of Guinea-Bissau, in the process of re-creation.

After the receipt of your letter we began again as a team to think more systematically about our collaboration with you. One conviction stood out, not only in relation to our past experiences but above all because of the political commitment to which we try to be loyal. Our conviction is that we will have nothing to teach there if we do not learn from and with you. For this reason, we go to Guinea-Bissau as comrades, as militants,* curiously and humbly, and not as foreign technicians with a mission. We do not judge ourselves to be the possessors of truth, nor do we carry with us a report of our visit already written or even drawn up in general lines with advice and prescriptions about what to do and how to do it. Such prescriptions could represent only

---

*Freire uses this term to designate persons actively committed to justice and liberation—political activists.—Translator.

what we had learned in other experiences in the past.

On the contrary, what our past and present experiences teach us is that they cannot ever be simply transplanted.

They can and must be explained, discussed and critically understood by those whose practice is in another context. In that new context they will be valid only to the degree that they are "reinvented."

In this way, the experience which has happened in context A becomes valuable as an example for context B only if those working there re-create it, thus refusing the temptation to perform a mechanical and alienating transplant. Being completely closed to experiences realized in other contexts is just as wrong as being ingenuously open to them, leading to pure and simple importation. Amilcar Cabral never denied the importance of experience in other contexts but he never accepted its blind imitation.

Thus, whenever we refer to this or that aspect of some other experience in which we have participated or know about, our intention will be to sharpen it as a problem statement or to offer a challenge.

Because this is the basis of our thinking and action, there is no place even for the outline of a project in the field of literacy education for adults in Guinea-Bissau in our reflections as a team. The project will have to be developed there, by you, in a process in which we may be able to collaborate, but only to the degree to which we come to know better the reality of the country.

Of course we can discuss here the complexities of adult literacy education, the impossibility of isolating it as something realizable above and beyond social practice within the society; we can discuss the necessity, for this very reason, for associating it with the overall concept of the society which one is attempting to create and of which the act of production is a fundamental dimension.

We can discuss, also, the political nature of literacy education as of all education, a fact that demands of educators a growing clarity regarding their own political stance, and the coherence of their practice with that stance.

We are thinking of the experience of the people in the older liberated zones of the country under the leadership of PAIGC in the fields of education, production, distribution and health. We are thinking, too, of the inherited colonial education that stands in complete contradiction to the society you are trying to create; it must be radically transformed and not simply reformed. The new educational system that is to come into being cannot be a happy synthesis of the inheritance of the liberation war and of the colonial legacy. It must be a deepening, improving and enriching of all of that—which means something new that results from the transformation of colonial education.

We have also thought of the difficulties such a radical transformation poses since it cannot be the fruit of a purely mechanical act.

We have considered how negative it would be for Guinea-Bissau, in the light of the political, social and cultural objectives that have always directed the practice of PAICG, simply to import an elitist model of education, generally called "higher education"—one that creates intellectualists and technocrats rather than intellectuals and technicians.

And it is true, therefore, that we see ourselves as comrades conversing frankly with comrades. We are ready to begin, with humility, our collaboration with the government of Guinea-Bissau and, above all, with the Commission on Education and Culture.

The concrete basis of this collaboration will be discussed there on the occasion of our first visit. From the dialogue between us, about the reality with which we will have had our first contact, will be born the program which will be carried out with our help.

Before that time comes, however, it is possible that I will be writing you again, reporting on our activities in Geneva.

*Fraternally,*
*Paulo Freire*

# Letter 3

Geneva
July 28, 1975

Engineer Mario Cabral
Commissioner of State for Education and Culture
Bissau, Republic of Guinea-Bissau

*Dear Comrade:*

Ever since last February when I wrote you for the first time about the possibility of a contribution by the Institute for Cultural Action (IDAC) in the field of literacy education for adults, an interest shared by the Department of Education of the WCC, we have been reflecting about this problem.

Since we do not see ourselves as foreign specialists, as I emphasized in my last letter, but rather as persons committed to the cause of Guinea-Bissau, it seems to us not only interesting but necessary to keep our comrade informed regarding some of our reflections. Therefore this letter-report is intended for that purpose and will, we hope, help all of us in the conversations we will have together there in September.

In our meetings in Geneva, our concerns have been around three interrelated areas:

a) A first attempt to become oriented to the reality of Guinea-Bissau by studying whatever materials we could obtain, especially the exceptional work of Amilcar Cabral.

b) Taking a critical distance from the different experiences of literacy education for adults in which we have taken part, directly or indirectly, in Brazil and elsewhere in Latin America. We have been thinking and rethinking the positive and negative aspects of these experiences. This exercise seemed fruitful to us as a means of learning from it in the face of the work to be done in Guinea-Bissau. We remember, however, what I emphasized in my last letter, that experiences are not transplanted, they are reinvented.

c) Imagining the role that literacy education for adults as cultural action could play in the construction of the new Guinea-Bissau.

Let me say again that this letter-report cannot pretend to touch on all of the points we have thought about and discussed in relation to the three areas noted above. It is more like a conversation between comrades and will actually be far less didactic and systematic than the first page suggests.

The climate that characterizes our study meetings is one of critical curiosity and of search. We challenge ourselves—at times to read a text of Amilcar Cabral, at others to relive different moments from our earlier experiences in the literacy education of adults.

These meetings, so far from Guinea-Bissau, are simply an introduction to our real apprenticeship. Without that apprenticeship our help would not be in the least useful. With our trip there, this apprenticeship will be continued more concretely.

The more we study the theoretical work of Amilcar Cabral the more we realize that we must return again and again to his works. They are an expression of his practical experiences with his people. His analyses of the role of culture in the struggle for liberation cannot be reduced to the historical moment of the war. That struggle—which was, as he said, both "a cultural fact and a factor of culture"—continues now, although in a different form. Yesterday the liberation struggle sought victory against the colonizer by means of the "liberation of the productive forces" from which would result "new perspectives on the cultural processes" of the country. Today, liberation is a continuing process. It signifies not only the consolidation of victory but also makes concrete a model of society already, in a certain sense, designed during the stage of struggle.

This model is, first of all, a political model. It will necessarily involve a total cultural project with education, including literacy education of adults, inherent within it. This is a cultural project which, being faithful to its popular roots without idealizing them, is faithful also to the struggle to increase production in the country.

A cultural action, even at the level of literacy education of adults, can accomplish a great deal. With reference to the struggle for production and committed to the increase of this production, the work of cultural action must go far beyond mechanical processes for literacy education or a purely technical training of peasants and urban workers. It must make a fundamental contribution to the political consciousness of the people. In a capitalist society the technical training of the so-called qualified work hands implies the suffocation of the workers' political consciousness. In Guinea-Bissau economic productivity will increase to the degree that the political consciousness of the popular masses becomes clarified.

It is in this sense that the ministry of education, in whatever society, is always an eminently political ministry. Politics serves the interests of the dominant class in a class society; it serves the interests of the people in a revolutionary society.

If we look at literacy education in this perspective, we can understand why it should never be looked at in isolation nor reduced to a set of techniques and methods. It is not that methods and techniques are not important. But they must serve the objectives contained in a cultural plan. This, in its turn, is involved in and involves the political and economic objectives in the concrete model of the society to be constructed. It is for this reason that in our training seminars for teachers we have not emphasized methods and techniques, but, rather, political clarity. This emphasis becomes even more important when we are talking about qualifying middle-class young people who have not yet committed the "class suicide" to which Amilcar Cabral refers and which he accomplished in so exemplary a manner.

Training seminars are really useful only insofar as they promote a unity of theory and practice giving emphasis to the ideological conditioning of class and to the necessity of "class suicide." By demonstrating the unity of theory and practice, they prepare students for the "suicide" that will become concrete when they are able to join the oppressed classes in the struggle for liberation. This is the case in Guinea-Bissau today where the people's struggle for the creation of the new society continues, even without war.

In a training seminar in Guinea-Bissau today it would be important, before analyzing any of the technical difficulties, to discuss certain affirmations of Amilcar Cabral such as the following:

> Other orators have had an opportunity to describe his character and to offer well-deserved eulogies to Dr. Edward Mondlane. We do not wish simply to reaffirm our admiration for this African patriot and for the eminent man of culture that he was. We have an equal desire to say that the great merit of Edward Mondlane was not in his decision to struggle for the liberation of his people. Rather, his greatest merit was to have known how to integrate himself with the reality of his country, with his people, and to develop his own cultural background through the struggle which he directed with such courage, wisdom and determination.

Or another of his references to the necessity for intellectuals to identify with the popular masses:

> A reconversion of the spirit and mentality (of the intellectuals) is indispensible for true integration within the liberation movement. Such a reconversion —or re-Africanization, in our case—can begin to operate before the struggle but it is not complete except in the course of the struggle itself, in daily contact with the masses and in the communion of sacrifice that the struggle requires.

Without the "reconversion" upon which Amilcar Cabral insisted so frequently, it is not possible for the middle-class intellectual to internalize the liberation struggle and to be integrated within it.

Without this reconversion it will never be possible for middle-class urban youths to participate with the peasants in the authentic cultural struggle for which adult literacy education is a starting point.

Without this reconversion, the tendency of the literacy worker is to try to alphabetize the learner, to transmit his own learning, to offer his own vision, often deformed by the urban experience. This kind of literacy education is not a creative act but a mechanical, bureaucratic one. It is often limited to the memorization of words and of sentences that almost never have anything to do with the reality of the learners.

"La, le, li, lo, lu; ba, be, bi, bo, bu; ta, te, ti, to, tu," says the educator committed to repetition and memorization. "Everyone with me," he continues. "Everyone together. Once more. Close your eyes. Once again."

From the ideology of his own class position, the educator, even when he verbalizes a revolutionary stance, does not perceive that to know is not to swallow knowledge. The act of teaching presupposes the act of learning and vice versa. If the educator takes refuge in his role as educator of the people without accepting his own need to be educated by the people, then his revolutionary oratory is counteracted by an alienating and reactionary practice. This aspect did not pass unperceived by Amilcar Cabral. He called attention to the fact that in the liberation movement all that glitters is not necessarily gold: leaders, politicians, even the most celebrated, can be culturally alienated.

In all of the experiments in which we have participated, in Brazil and in other places, we have confronted this problem.

We have observed, for example, that at the intellectual level the teachers in a training seminar may accept totally our analysis of the literacy education of adults as a creative act. They might agree that the learners should assume the role of Subjects in the process of learning their own language and of the expression of that language. Indeed they might understand and accept intellectually that their role as teachers should not be that of transferring knowledge as though they knew everything and the learners knew nothing. They might even be able to apply certain methodological procedures coherent with these principles.

In actual practice, however, many of these teachers are conditioned by their class position and by the myths of their superiority in relation to the peasants and workers. They assimilate these myths during their own class education and reduce the learners to mere depositories for their knowledge. Instead of challenging the peasants to "read" their reality, they offer discourses to the peasants in a language that they are unable to understand.

Their methodological errors have ideological roots. To correct them requires more than insistence on the methods themselves. It requires a permanent revision of the ideological class conditioning of teachers.

Therefore we insist increasingly, in the qualifying seminars, on analysis of national reality, on the political clarity of the educator, on the understanding of ideological conditioning, and on the perception of cultural differences. All this must begin long before discussion of literacy techniques and methods. Literacy must come together with its practice.

Another problem we have encountered has been that of reconciling this necessity for basic orientation with the requirement of qualifying a large number of teachers as rapidly as possible. We have come to the conclusion—although we have not been able to generalize it—that the ideal would be to begin training fifteen persons. When these fifteen were in the midst of their course, we would institute 15 "Culture Circles" with 20 learners in each one. We would make it very clear to the 300 learners that their contribution would have great importance. They would not be coming to the Culture Circles simply to receive "letters" passively as though these were a gift from the teacher. They would be coming to the Culture Circles to help the teachers become teachers. Without them, this learning could not take place. Thus, from the beginning, the learners would be called upon to assume the role of Subjects in the process of their own learning, in the course of which they would also have something to teach. At the same time, this direct contact between those who were becoming literate and the literacy teachers would constitute the basis for the teachers' reflection on their immediate experience, thus achieving a unity between theory and practice.

When these 15 were coming to the—apparent—end of the training, we would begin with 15 more. These would have an advantage over the first group since they would already be starting with a unity of theory and practice. From the beginning they would be able to observe and reflect on the experience of the first group. Some days later, another 15 Culture Circles would be formed with another 300 learners, with whom the same discussion would be held as that described above.

The exchange of experiences between the first two groups would be of extreme importance. From among them the training team would choose other training squads. Thus the program could be multiplied and intensified.

By then, with 30 involved in the ongoing process, we would receive 30 more who would continue in the same rhythm; later, 60, and after that, 100.

Even though this practice has not become generalized, it has been successful wherever it has been tried.

Another point we have been concerned about in our reflections in Geneva is that of making use of persons from the locality itself for the work of popular education. Some of the best experiments I have seen were those in Chile where we had as educators young Chilean peasants who, when they were trained, revealed indisputable efficiency. They worked in the rural areas, participating in production, which was not for them something vague. They were a group of young people who were not dreaming of how they might become urbanized. Their dreams were fully identified with those of their own communities.

Supported by these experiments in which I took part and by the analysis of others in which I did not participate—even recognizing that experience cannot be transplanted but must be reinvented–I put forth this hypothesis:

If it were not possible either to count on peasants who can be rapidly trained for literacy work, as in Chile, nor on urban youths capable of committing "class suicide" and of "knowing how to become integrated into their country and with their people," then I would rather dedicate the necessarily longer time to train peasants who might become authentic educators of their comrades, than to use middle-class youth. The latter may be trained more rapidly but their commitment is less trustworthy.

I have not referred in this letter to one very important concern: linguistics. Such is the complexity of this subject that we prefer to discuss it with you personally.

We await the arrival of Comrade Edna Pereira after the 20th of August. I would ask you, please, to confirm the day of her arrival.

*With the cordial embrace of*
*Paulo Freire*

# Letter 4

Geneva
August 1975

Engineer Mario Cabral
Commissioner of State for Education and Culture
Bissau, Republic of Guinea-Bissau

*Comrade Mario Cabral,*
    Just a few words to tell you how important we felt the meeting was which we had with Comrade Theobald, who came because Comrade Edna was unable to be with us as we had hoped.

We were impressed with the assurance of his replies to our inquiries, not only about the activities going on in education, production, distribution and health in the older liberated zones of Guinea-Bissau, but also about all that you are trying to do today in the phase of national reconstruction.

We are certain that the conversations we had with him during the four days will help us immensely in our preparation for the visit that we will make to your country next month. We gleaned rich information from these conversations. They became the climax of the systematic studies we have been carrying on since last February in preparation for our first direct contact with the reality of Guinea-Bissau.

In the next few days you will be receiving a letter from IDAC in which we will make a few suggestions about the organization of our program of work with you there in September.

*Fraternally,*
*Paulo Freire*

# Letter 5

Geneva
October 1975

Engineer Mario Cabral
Commissioner of State for Education and Culture
Bissau, Republic of Guinea-Bissau

*Comrade Mario Cabral,*
Having just arrived from there, I write you not only to thank you and your comrades with whom we worked during our stay for the fraternal manner in which you received us; we also want to reaffirm the satisfaction that we felt at being able, in dialogue with all of you, to establish the basis for the small contribution that we may be able to make to the Commission on Education of Guinea-Bissau.

Our interaction with you and the first contact with the reality of your country solidified in us the commitment with which we began our journey there. In truth, it is we who must thank you for the opportunity to work with you as comrades, taking part in the effort to re-create Guinea-Bissau.

Elza and I were also moved by the discussion in the Culture Circles of FARP in which the participants, writing sentences on the blackboard, discussed clearly the theme to which they referred.

We knew that we were in a Culture Circle in Bissau but, in a certain sense, it was as though we were back in Brazil in years gone by, learning from and with the students, not only teaching them.

We were moved by what we heard, and by what we saw, but we were not surprised at the clear understanding of politics revealed in the debates. The same clarity was shown by the teams of the Commission on Education when they discussed with us the general situation of education. This clarity tends to become greater as the teams confront the problems to be resolved—with no pretence at becoming specialists in the matter.

We all know—both you and we—how much remains to be done to place national education at the service of the new society that is being created. We all know—you and we—that such an undertaking, since it is not the result of a mechanical act, implies a radical transformation in the system of colonial education, and without this the whole plan for a new society could be frustrated.

We will always need to return to this fundamental theme which was the object of our discussions there. It is, as I suggested in my first letter, simply not possible to discuss literacy as a process in itself. (In fact, we would accomplish little if we were to develop a literacy program that, while correct in itself, still preserved, as you noted last week, the elitist, verbal characteristics of the present system.)

What lies ahead to be done constitutes a challenge, in response to which it is our intention to become, with you, truly engaged.

With this goes the friendly embrace for all of you of

*Paulo Freire*

# Letter 6

Geneva
November 26, 1975

Engineer Mario Cabral
Commissioner of State for Education and Culture
Bissau, Republic of Guinea-Bissau

*Dear Comrade Mario,*

I am writing once again, even before receiving your reply to the letter to which all of us on the team signed our names and in which we communicated to you the fact that we had obtained the financing that will make our work together in Guinea-Bissau possible. We also proposed February for our first visit in 1976. The purpose of this letter is to tell you something of what we have been doing in Geneva in the light of our work together in Guinea-Bissau.

We have been continuing our studies as a team—two meetings a week in addition to what each of us does along these lines alone. We are deepening our understanding of the essence of the problem of Guinea-Bissau. At the same time we have been thinking about the preparation of some material that might be useful for you, but which, nonetheless, you would need to test. We are also collecting documentation regarding literacy which we will send to the Commission.

There is growing interest in Europe about everything that goes on in Guinea-Bissau. In different meetings in Paris, Stockholm and Geneva, members of the team have spoken about the plans for the work in which we are involved with you.

The letter, a copy of which I enclose, is one of several that we will be sending to the team in Bissau. Although I realize the vast amount of work that you have, it would really be wonderful if the team were able to speed up somewhat its work on the manual for facilitators and give itself especially to preparing material, as suggested in the attached letter.

I do not know whether it would be too much to ask you to meet with the team and to spend a bit of time talking with them about the letter, discussing the most efficient ways to produce the material about which the letter speaks.

An embrace for Comrade Beatrice and for all of the comrades, our friends. Special love to Panau from all of us.

*Fraternally,*
*Paulo Freire*

# Letter 7

Geneva
November 26, 1975

*Comrades Monica, Edna and Paulo,*

In our earlier letter to Comrade Mario Cabral, in which we sent concrete word of our work here toward the continuity of our common task, we said that other letters would follow, written by one or the other of us, regarding specific points in the action program.

What we are writing now is specifically related to the material necessary for the use of projectors and recorders which will be sent directly to Bissau for preserving the debates in the Culture Circles.

The material should be used in Culture Circles whose location is obviously up to you to decide, in accordance with whatever the real situation there indicates. We believe it would be interesting to carry out the experiment not only within FARP but also in a heavily populated area in Bissau with civilian learners. In this way we could compare results, not only from the point of view of learning to read and write more or less rapidly, but also of the content of the discussions of both these groups

—the levels of greater or less critical perception of local and national reality, for example.

The preparation of material for the projectors will require even more of you than you are already doing so well in organizing the programmatic content for literacy work. Already you have made a selection of the generative words, having in mind their political and sociological richness as well as their phonetic structure. The use of the projectors will now require some codes in which the generative words will be included.

Before going further in this letter, I want to say parenthetically that the theoretical considerations that I shall offer result from critical reflection on my own experience or on that of others which I have analyzed over the years: they are not offered as dogma. You will not only be able to, but indeed must, re-create what has been done in the field of literacy education for adults—where there is a whole world of things to be thought about and thought about again.

Let us return to the problem of coding, in which the generative words are to be included. Perhaps it would be useful to take it now as an object of critical analysis, discussing, above all, its role in a liberating, educational praxis. When I say in a liberating educational praxis, I am highlighting the impossibility of neutral coding (or decoding). An educationally dominating approach also uses codes, the constitution and the objectives of which are different from these found in a liberating educational praxis. The learners are forced to assume a quite different posture.

It may be interesting also not to start with a definition—which is always difficult—of coding. Instead you might try to understand by means of reflection what we all do in our own actions as educators influenced by the revolutionary nature of our particular political stance.

Education, cultural action, animation—the name doesn't matter—always implies, at the level of literacy and post-literacy, a theory of knowledge put in practice and a way of knowing. One of the first questions that we have to ask, therefore, is about this theory itself and the object to be known (which constitutes the programmatic content of education, literacy and post-literacy work).

In the first place, the theory of knowledge that serves a revolutionary objective and is put into practice in education is based upon the claim that knowledge is always a process, and results from the conscious action (practice) of human beings on the objective reality which, in its turn, conditions them. Thus a dynamic and contradictory unity is established between objective reality and the persons acting on it. All reality is dynamic and contradictory in this same way.

From the point of view of such a theory and of the education which grows from it, it is not possible:

a) to separate theory and practice;
b) to separate the act of knowing existing knowledge from the act of creating new knowledge;
c) to separate teaching from learning, educating from being educated.

The method coherent with this theory of knowledge is itself as dynamic as the object to be known—objective reality.

When we are dealing with social practice in which the struggle for production, class conflict, and creative action are all dynamically interrelated, we discover that education is a process that takes social practice as the basis for learning and study. Education is itself a dimension of social practice. It seeks to know the reason for the practice and, through this knowledge as it deepens and develops, it also seeks new practice that is consistent with the overall plan for the society.

It is in the deepening and diversification—never narrowly specialized or focused—of this knowledge that the starting point of post-literacy is found. This, like the act of knowing, is not something separate from literacy training itself, but its logical continuity. In this way, post-literacy finds itself already known (announced) in literacy education. In this, the learning to read and write, necessarily associated with the development of the ability to express oneself, grows with the use of dynamic methods through which the teacher and learner alike seek to understand the social practice in critical terms. The learning of reading and writing involves also learning to "read" reality by means of the correct analysis of social practice.

In this phase, discussion of aspects of social practice, like those of production, for example, provide the opportunity to touch on technical points regarding the why and how of these practices.

In post-literacy work, the reading of reality continues in a deeper form. However, it now stresses a more technical and specialized knowledge, including a greater mastery of language, a sharper perception of economic and social organization, as well as an understanding of history, geography and mathematics.

We have spoken before of the impossibility of separating practice from theory. A society that seeks to live the radical unity between the two overcomes the dichotomy between manual labor and intellectual labor. The result is a totally different model of education. In this model, the school—whether primary, secondary or university level—is not essentially different from the factory or the farm, nor does it stand in opposition to them. Even when a school exists outside the factory or the practical tasks of agriculture, this does not signify that it is in any way superior to them, nor that factory or agricultural work are not in themselves schools also. In a dynamic vision of the unity between theory and practice, the school, inside or outside the factory, cannot be defined as an institution bureaucratically responsible for the transfer of a select kind of knowledge. It is rather a pole or moment of that unity. Thus, distancing ourselves from the concrete practice, wherever we exercise critical reflection about that practice, we have there a theoretical context, a school, that is, in the most radical sense which that word should have.

In order to use the projectors we are sending, you will need to make the codifications yourselves. These codings represent aspects of reality; they express moments in the concrete context. In this way they provide a link between the concrete and the theoretical context—in our situation, the Culture Circle. They also relate the educator and the learner as active Subjects seeking to learn together. In this dynamic view, the coding is not simply an aid for the teacher that helps him/her teach better but is an object of learning that challenges the learner.

Depending on the channel of communication to be used, the coding can be: visual; auditory; tactile; or audio-visual.

The visual can be:

a) pictorial: a painting, a drawing, or a photograph;

b) printed, written language;

c) pantomine or mime,* i.e., expressions of thought by means of gestures and action.

The coding may be simple or complex, according to whether one channel of communication is to be used or several simultaneously. With reference to language, not even necessarily written, all coding is a discourse to be read. In this sense, it has a superficial structure and a profound structure in dynamic relation with each other. The surface structure is a set of elements which, in interaction, make it up. The deeper structure is not visible; it emerges to the degree that the reading or decoding of the code—or, more precisely, of the surface structure—extends vertically. It has to do with the essential rationale for the facts which are merely exposed, but not truly revealed, in the superstructure. Perhaps we can understand better the surface structure and the deeper structure of any coding if we think of the difference between the grammar and the syntax of the same text. Let us take, for example, the following text from the point of view of grammar and then of syntax: "I desire that you do good work."

In a purely grammatical reading of the text, my preoccupation would be to take all of its parts by themselves and to classify them. My behavior would be that of a taxonomist. Thus, I would say:

"I desire": a verb, first-person singular, of the present tense, indicative mood;

---

*I am interested in the potential that pantomime, as a bodily expression, might have in cultures in which the body has not been submerged in a rationalizing intellectualism. In these cultures, the great majority has not yet been subjected to the logical precision of written language from which, frequently, emerged a myth about the power of this language. (For our part, we try to avoid this myth from the very first stage of literacy education.) In these cultures, the body has great freedom in its relations with nature and moves easily in accord with its own myths. It would be interesting to think in terms of games of pantomime as coding and, in the pictorial codes, to give emphasis to movement. I raise this question simply as an inquiry which could perhaps in the future open up for us certain lines of study.

"that": a conjunction used to introduce a subordinate
    clause stating a wish;
"you": pronoun, second-person singular or plural;
"do": verb, present tense, subjunctive use;
"good": adjective;
"work": noun, object of verb, etc.

From the point of view of the syntax, my behavior would be completely different. In this case, my concern would be to understand the text as a whole, defining its interacting parts as they constitute the totality. I would seek to perceive the role the words play in the general structure of the text. In this way, I would recognize the complementary relation that exists between "good work" and "I desire." In this sense "you do good work" is the object, the direct complement of "I desire," which is the expression of a certain incomplete state, a transitive verb. The first phrase has as its subject "I"; the complementary phrase has as its subject "you," and so on.

In the analysis of syntax, thus, the classification that is made is not of the words in themselves, but of the functions they have in relation to each other, in the general structure of their context which expresses a structured thought.

If we take the coding that represents men and women working in the fields (a photograph or drawing), the superficial structure will be made up of those elements that are immediately perceived; the basic structure will come into focus when, deepening the analysis of the superstructure, we seek the reason for the coded fact: Why are they working? Who are they?

The reaction of one who comes in contact for the first time with the process of coding is to read the superstructure. Such a reading is purely grammatical or taxonomical, we might say, in which the coded elements are described. When we start with this manner of reading, moreover, and then seek to go on to a deeper level of the coding, the educator must not press his own position to the point that the learners' position is a mere reflection of his own. At the same time, the educator must not negate, as though from shame, his own insights.

If we have a critical understanding of both the superficial and the deeper structures of coding, we can, in the act of constructing our own codes, defend ourselves against two risks. The first danger is that we may reduce the coding simply to a message to be transmitted when it is, in reality, an object to be known, even a challenge, a problem to be revealed. The second danger is that we may transform the code into some kind of puzzle to be solved.

In the first case, the code, in becoming so closely identified with the message, also becomes so explicit that the struggle to decode it is almost unnecessary. The coding is almost decoded within itself. The coding represented by propaganda (advertising) is an illustration of what I have just said. Its message merely domesticates the one who reads it.

In the second case, the superstructure of the coding is so enigmatic and closed in its form that obstacles are placed in the way of the decoding process.

From the point of view of style, the coding can in either case be comical or humorous. However, when they invoke laughter and relaxation, having a cathartic effect, they can be distinguished from each other. When the message is too obvious, it leaves the one who is attempting to decode it at the level of the superstructure. When the coding is enigmatic, humor may facilitate reaching the deeper structure of the coding.*

## Coding and Generative Words

Once you have chosen the generative words, using the criteria with which you are already familiar, it is time to elaborate the coding in which they will be included. There is a necessary relationship between the generative words and the coding. Sometimes it is between the word and the coding as a whole. Sometimes only a word is to be abstracted from the coding.

An example of coding that refers to the whole:
  Generative Word: "work".
  Coding: men and women working.
An example of a word to be found in the coding:
  Generative Word: "brick"

---

*The work of the cartoonist Claudius Ceccon is a good example of the second case.

Coding: men working on a construction project in which bricks are clearly in the foregound.

Your work, therefore, is to prepare material in which the coding corresponds to the 17 generative words that will constitute the literacy program for the experimental circles.

I am sending you, as an example, a set of slides that we used in Brazil, with the generative word in the corresponding coding and the slide in which the word appears broken down into syllables.

I shall also send another series of Brazilian slides. This set was produced on education as action expressive of freedom. In the Brazilian experience this material opened up the discussion on the concept of culture. This discussion, in the last analysis, is part of a critical apprehension of the relations between human beings and the natural world. From the transformation of this natural world the specifically human world of culture and of history emerges.

In Brazil this discussion preceded literacy work and continued parallel with it. In Chile, chiefly because the learners were so eager to begin immediately to learn to read and write, the discussion of culture took place during the literacy process. The important thing is that such an analysis take place.

You may find it interesting to test some of the Brazilian codings—those that are closest to your local reality—with some of your groups of learners and to study their reaction.

If you do make such a test, it will be important to record the discussions so that the team there can analyze them critically. In our next visit to Guinea-Bissau, one of the work sessions could center on the study of these recordings as well as on the multiple use of the conversations of the learners. We spoke of this last September when we were with you.

Another point we could work on together in Bissau next February, if Comrade Mario Cabral confirms the proposed dates, is how to motivate the learners so that they will also be able to do some coding in teams. Each team would then lead the discussion of their own codings.

As soon as we have received the material from you—the codings and the generative words broken down—we will make the sets of slides for the program of the reading circles.

Finally, within the next few days, we will send you a photo-copy of the text of a book of mine to be published next year about which I spoke to you when I was there. Some of it may interest you. You will find something about the problem of coding, for example, in *Cultural Action for Freedom* and in *Pedagogy of the Oppressed* also.

Receive the affectionate embrace of all of us.

*Paulo Freire*

# Letter 8

Geneva
December 6, 1975

Engineer Mario Cabral
Commissioner of State for Education and Culture
Bissau, Republic of Guinea-Bissau

*Comrade Mario Cabral,*

I received your letter several days ago. You report receiving mine in which I told you I have obtained funds from the CCPD to continue our work, and also a contribution from the Depart-ment of Education of the WCC. So I am now in a position to be of service to the project.

I hope that the letter I wrote last month, to which I appended copies for Monica, Edna and Paulo, has also arrived.

Today I am sending you a copy of another letter I have just finished writing to them. I feel as though you should always be aware of correspondence that goes to the team in Bissau, thus accompanying the steps which we are taking.

Have you been able, despite the intensity of all your other

work, to install the National Commission which will, with you, be responsible for the general policies of the national campaign of literacy? It would be great if, in our next visit in February 1976, we could meet at least once with that commission.

My dear friend, pardon these insistences. They are made in the desire to be of service.

For you and all of the comrades, an embrace from your friend,

*Paulo Freire*

# Letter 9

Geneva
December 6, 1975

*Dear Comrades and Friends, Monica, Edna and Paulo,*

I hope that you received the letter that I sent you through Comrade Mario Cabral in which I spoke of the process of coding for the experiments there in which you will be using projectors. I also hope that your work on the manual for facilitators is going forward and that we shall be receiving copies soon.

We know how busy you are but we would really be interested in a report of all that has happened since our visit in Bissau: the carrying out of activities in FARP; whether the new coordinators, who were being trained when we were there, are already in action; and whether their work goes well.

If my memory is correct, I believe that Marcos Arruda made a similar request in his recent letter.

I wonder whether you are able to hold systematic evaluation seminars with the leaders in which you and they examine the experience of all—the difficulties you have met and the manner in which you have attempted to respond to these. Certain difficulties are always repeated; it is important that all of the leaders become informed about how the others confront these. This makes for a common learning base that stimulates the creativity of all.

In these seminars, for example, some of the authoritarian tendencies of some of the facilitators as well as some of the unexpected mistakes of others can be considered. None of these errors can be completely avoided unless we are working with only ten or 15 persons, which for us, in this situation, does not make sense.

These evaluation seminars can also include some of the learners. Their presence can be justified on two basic grounds: what is being discussed in these seminars is something in which they are involved as Subjects just as the coordinators are; also, through such meetings the training process can be deepened. Among the learners are tomorrow's facilitators. The manual you are preparing should itself pass through the critical appraisal of such seminars.

If you have not yet thought of this kind of activity but agree that it is one that ought to be undertaken, the question is one of finding the best way to make it operational. Be sure to record the conversations. The record of the conversations constitutes, in itself, an important document. It allows you to study the progress of the work and it can also be used in the evaluation seminars of different groups.

The task of evaluation is a means of training and, as such, is intimately linked to the search for new forms of action. Looking at one's own practice as a problem provides the critical moment in evaluation. The subjects of the practice can thus go back over what has been done in order to confirm or to rectify it in this or that aspect, enriching subsequent practice and being enriched by it. This is why we feel the necessity, whenever we participate in a central team, not only to accompany closely the activities of the Culture Circles, but also to connect, from time to time, with the discussions that go on in them. In this way, our participation in the evaluation seminars where the work of the Culture Circles is the object of analysis will not be the participation of strangers to the practice, nor of semi-involved persons, that is, as those who have simply watched how others work.

It is possible, of course, that you have already used, or are thinking of using, methods of evaluation somewhat different from these. That is not important. The important thing is, first, that there be ongoing evaluation of the work being realized and, second, that the evaluation never become a type of fiscalization.

I am sending, by airmail, the texts that I promised. I know you will read them with the reality of Guinea-Bissau as a point of reference.

We await news from you.

*With the embrace of,*
*Paulo Freire*

# Letter 10

Geneva
January 5, 1976

Engineer Mario Cabral
Commissioner of State for Education and Culture
Bissau, Guinea-Bissau

*Comrade Mario,*
Once again I am sending you copies of another letter, very long this time, that I have written to Comrades Monica, Edna and Paulo.

I believe that the theme I have treated has a lot to do with Guinea-Bissau although that need not mean that you agree completely with what I have said.

It might be interesting to discuss the principal points with the team in February.

I am also sending an extra copy with yours that you might give to Comrade Dulce whose responsibility is middle level instruction. I think it possible that the letter might interest her also.

We are anxious to arrive there and to see you all again and to drink in some of that joy in living, something that is rather lacking around here.

*An embrace for all,*
*Paulo Freire*

# Letter 11

Geneva
January 5, 1976

*Comrades Monica, Edna and Paulo,*

Although it may not be necessary, it may in any case be well to say that in writing more or less assiduously to you I do not pretend either to bureaucratize our relationship nor to give to my letters any prescriptive significance. I write only because I must talk with you about points that interest us in view of the work in which we are all engaged.

In writing, naturally, I have in mind to challenge you; but, in doing so, I challenge myself also. It is not possible to challenge anyone authentically, without, at the same time, addressing the challenge also to ourselves. Sometimes I pause over a word or phrase, asking myself whether what I am writing truly expresses what I want to say and whether, above all, it is rooted in the concrete reality about which I am thinking.

Today I would like to touch on some of the problems that confront us when, involved in the practice and the theory of adult literacy education, we ask ourselves what will follow after it.

I do not intend a detailed analysis of post-literacy, but simply to establish a stance in relation to it which corresponds to the vision that I have of literacy. As a matter of fact, concerns about post-literacy work are intimately related to the conception one has of literacy education itself.

Each time I have discussed literacy education for adults, I have stressed that, in the perspective of liberation, it must always be a creative act in which undisciplined knowing gives way to a form of knowledge that emerges from critical reflection on the concrete practice of work. Hence the insistence with which I always speak of the dialectical relationship between the concrete context in which the practice takes place and the theoretical context in which critical reflection is done.

In such a vision, which is both practical and theoretical, literacy education can never be understood as a moment of formal learning of reading and writing, or as a primary instance of linking them to what is to follow. Nor should it be viewed as a kind of treatment to be applied to those who need it in order that they may be quickly cured of their infirmity, so that they may take part in some superior, if equally undisciplined, adventure known as post-literacy.

As I understand it, literacy education for adults contains within itself the elements of post-literacy. This continues and becomes deeper and more diversified, as the act of knowing in which it began. Literacy and post-literacy are not, therefore, two separate processes, one before and one later, but two moments of the same process of social formation. And it does not matter what name you give to it—"education," "cultural action," "motivation"—it always implies literacy and post-literacy. It is a theory of knowledge put into practice.

Education as an act of knowing confronts us with a number of theoretical-practical, not intellectual, questions: What to know? How to know? Why to know? In benefit of what and of whom to know? Moreover, against what and whom to know? These are fundamental questions, in dynamic relationship to others around the act of educating, its possibilities, its legitimacy, its objectives and ends, its agents, its methods and content.

All of these closely interwoven questions demand replies that are also interrelated. Thus, in concerning myself with what should be known, I am also necessarily involved with why it needs to be known, how, in benefit of what and in whose interest, as well as against what and whom.

The objective of this letter is not to study these questions

A school in the liberated zone during the period of the struggle for liberation. (Publication authorized by the Commission of Information and Tourism of the Republic of Guinea-Bissau)

A school in the liberated zone during the period of the struggle for liberation. (Publication authorized by the Commission of Information and Tourism of the Republic of Guinea-Bissau)

Defense against aerial attacks during the struggle for liberation. (Publication authorized by the Commission of Information and Tourism of the Republic of Guinea-Bissau)

Partial view of the Maxim Gorki Training Center, the school at Có, during recreation. (Photograph from Centro Audio-Visual, Guinea-Bissau)

A group of teachers, studying at the school at Có, working in the fields. (Photograph from Centro Audio-Visual, Guinea-Bissau)

Students from the Lycée of Bissau on their way to the fields to take part in productive labor. (Photograph from Centro Audio-Visual, Guinea-Bissau)

Students from the Lycée of Bissau participating in productive labor. (Photograph from Centro Audio-Visual, Guinea-Bissau)

Amilcar Cabral with a child in his arms. (Publication authorized by the Commission of Information and Tourism of the Republic of Guinea-Bissau)

The swearing-in of the Directors of PAIGC at the moment of the Declaration of Independence of the Republic of Guinea-Bissau. Medina de Boé, September 1973. At the center, President Luiz Cabral. (Publication authorized by the Commission of Information and Tourism of the Republic of Guinea-Bissau)

systematically and profoundly, but simply to call attention to them and to say a bit about them.

The reply to the question of what to know has to do directly with development of programmatic content of education and involves a number of aspects that cannot be neglected. The "why" is intimately related to all the other questions: How? To the benefit of what? In whose interest? Against what? Against whom? These are all at the very center of the definition of what to know.

The definition of what to know—without which it is not possible to organize the programmatic content of educational activity—is also intimately related to the overall plan for the society, to the priorities this plan requires, and to the concrete conditions for its realization.

In speaking of the plan for society, I do not suggest it as an abstract idea, an arbitrary design, something completed in the imagination of the leadership. I refer to certain goals which are closely related to each other. They are also coherent with specific objectives in a number of areas: economic and social organization; internal distribution as well as external trade; communication and transport; culture; health, education in general. Goals may be realizable in stages and should involve the politics of overall planning and the specific politics for realizing them.

In the effort to make the goals concrete, the design of the plan may have to be altered somewhat in actual practice. But these alterations cannot negate the overall vision of the plan. Defining what needs to be known in order to organize the content of educational activities demands political clarity of everyone involved in any part of the planning. This political clarity, though not sufficient by itself, is absolutely essential with regard to all the questions that need to be asked: For what reason? Why? And in whose interest do the policies themselves serve? Policies carried out by a rigid bureaucracy in the name of the masses to whom they are transmitted as order are one thing; policies carried out *with* the masses are quite another thing—with their critically conscious participation in the reconstruction of society, in which the necessary directions never become slogans.

It is this political clarity in the face of reality and of education itself that helps us to avoid the risk of reducing the organization of the curriculum to a set of neutral technical procedures. It is a clarity associated with being constantly vigilant so as to preserve the coherence between our practice and the plan for the new society. The organization of the programmatic content of education—whether it be primary, secondary, university, or at the level of a literacy campaign for adults—is an eminently political act, just as politics is an attitude which we assume in the choice of the techniques and methods for the concrete accomplishment of the task. The political character of all of this is independent of our consciousness of it. The knowledge of how to define what needs to be known cannot be separated from the *why* of knowing or from the other implications of this act to which I have referred. For this reason, there are no neutral specialists, no owners of neutral techniques in the field of curriculum organization—or in any other field, for that matter. There are no neutral "methodologists" who can teach how to teach history, geography, language or mathematics neutrally.

The definition of what needs to be known for the organization of the programmatic content of education is one of the most important tasks in a society moving from colonial dependence to a revolutionary struggle for its reconstruction. This definition regarding what to know is not completed, however, by substituting one kind of programmatic content for a content that corresponds more closely to the objectives of the society in reconstruction. Although during a certain period this effort is, sometimes, the only possible one, it is essential to understand that changing the programmatic content is not sufficient if earlier practice is simply modified in this or that aspect while the method of knowing remains elitist.

Preserving the elitist character of education, with all that implies, may make sense in a society that is moving from colonial dependence into neocolonial dependence, and is governed by a dominant national elite closely tied into the imperialist interests. This, however, without the shadow of a doubt, can never be said to be the case of Guinea-Bissau.

The basic challenge is not simply to substitute a new program for an old one that was adequate to the interests of the colonizers. It is to establish a coherence between the society that is being reconstructed in a revolutionary way and the education as a whole that is to serve that revolutionary society. And the theory of knowledge which the new society must put in practice requires a new way of knowing that is antagonistic to colonial education.

One of the risks such a society runs, as it attempts to reply to the challenge its reconstruction places before it, is to accept certain Western models. Among these, of course, is the educational model produced in a class society. It is never possible with middle-school and university degrees to develop national leaders able to undertake the enormous and complex task of revolutionary reconstruction.

This risk is very real for a society that seeks to remake itself in a revolutionary manner. Thus, the challenge for such a society is to find the correct route to combat the antipopular leadership style that has surrendered to the interests of imperialist control.

Admitting that the colonizer offered some opportunity for persons to gain university qualifications, this action was taken by the colonial power in its own interest. What was offered was selective and narrow, like the education that evolved in the urban schools in the colonial era.

Reaching only a small segment of the population, this university training would reinforce the status of its graduates who would simply increase the ranks of urban intellectuals in the service of the colonizers. Amilcar Cabral, in analyzing the role of a small group of these intellectuals in the struggle for liberation of their countries, referred to the necessity of their committing suicide as a class if they would be born again as revolutionary workers entirely identified with the most profound aspirations of their people.[1] The re-Africanization of these intellectuals about which Amilcar also insisted was implicit in this concept of death and rebirth.

It happens, however, that this "death" is not easily accepted, even by those verbally committed to a revolutionary stance. The intellectual training of the middle class reinforces the class position of individuals and tends to make them absolutize the validity of their own activity, which they consider superior to that of those without the same opportunities.

Every time the revolutionary leadership limits the field of, for example, scientific investigation—suppressing some activity the immediate results of which do not correspond to the most pressing needs of the great majority of the population—these intellectuals feel themselves discriminated against and without their freedom.

In this sense, there is much to be studied, done and redone in Guinea-Bissau before an investigator will be able to carry out a scientific analysis of why that dearly loved animal we have in Brazil, and certainly in Guinea-Bissau, called Laziness moves so slowly. There is a lot of work to be done in Guinea-Bissau collecting tales and stories of the people to be used as reading texts for children and adults, before some erudite professor of literature need be called to "give" seminars on Mallarmé or on the school of symbolism.

In the last analysis, I am convinced that it is easier to create a new type of intellectual—forged in the unity between practice and theory, manual and intellectual work—than to reeducate an elitist intellectual. When I say it is easier, I do not discount the validity of such reeducation when it does occur.

The challenge for such a society is not to continue creating elitist intellectuals so that they can commit suicide, but rather to prevent their formation in the first place. The preparation of cadres with a popular rather than an elitist orientation can be carried on not only outside but inside the country. Needs of learners can be defined in close relation to new pedagogical methods. In the final analysis, the reorientation of the educational system can overcome totally the colonial inheritance. It demands different objectives, different content, different practice, and a different conception of education.

The definition of what should be learned—even at the level of literacy education for adults—and the creation of programmatic content cannot be thought of apart from the reorientation of the educational system so that it is consistent with the plan for a new society. If the educational system follows an elitist verbal and auditory model that satisfies the interests of the colonizers—even though it may be reformed at this or that point —then literacy education for adults, whatever its particular orientation, will turn out to be the means of access for a few to the privileges which the system is set up to defend.

Thus discussion of adult literacy and post-literacy education implies a discussion of the whole field of education in the society. And to discuss education, I repeat, is to think of the overall plan for the society itself.

Colonial education has as one of its principal objectives—parallel with the de-Africanization of the national population—the preparation of lower-level administrators. Now what is important is the formation of new men and women, and, as part of that process, the creation of that new type of intellectual to which I referred above. And it is not on the basis of what the society inherited from the colonizers that this task can be accomplished.

Vigilance as a permanent attitude in a society that seeks to transform itself has a key role: "In the area of culture, as in politics," said Cabral, "vigilance is indispensable."[2] Lack of vigilance can be fatal to the plan for the new society. And if the society, in remaking itself, moves toward socialism, it needs, on the one hand, to organize its methods of production with this objective in mind, and, on the other, to structure its education in close relation to production, both from the point of view of the understanding of the productive process and also the technical training of the learners.

In this sense, the new man and the new woman toward which this society aspires cannot be created except by participation in productive labor that serves the common good. It is this labor that is the source of knowledge about this new creation, through which it unfolds and to which it refers. Such education, then, cannot be elitist in character because this would lead, in contradiction to the socialist objectives, to strengthening the division between manual and mental labor. It is necessary, rather, to overcome this dichotomy in order that, in the new education, the primary school, the secondary school and the university cannot be distinguished, essentially, from the factory or from the productive activity in the agricultural field. Nor is it placed in opposition to them. And even when, as in its theoretical context, the education takes place outside the factory and agricultural activity, this does not mean that it should be considered as superior to them, nor that they are not also schools.

In the dynamic vision of the unity between practice and theory the school can never be defined as a bureaucratic institution responsible for the transfer of a select knowledge. Nor can it be defined as a "market" for learning. It is necessary, moreover, that the dichotomy between manual and mental labor, between practice and theory, be overcome. This, further, must be extended to include also the dichotomy between teaching and learning and between the knowledge that exists today and creating new knowledge. With the overcoming of these dichotomies, the school as a "market for knowledge" is superseded by the school as a democratic learning center, as Comrade Samora Machel has suggested.

In such a school, the authoritarian teacher who transmits select learning disappears; so also does the passive student who receives this learning. In their place, as Machel also pointed out, arise active teachers and learners: teachers who, in teaching, also learn, and students who, in learning, also teach.

An education like this is in harmony with a social plan that rewards the presence of peasants and urban workers who are increasingly conscious of their role in the reconstruction of the society. In such an education, defining what should be known must count on the involvement of the learners as part of the plan. This means that the dialogic relation, as a seal of the act of knowing, between active teachers and learners is not the result of some objective of learning proposed by the professor to the learners but arises in response to the definition of what needs to be known.

Without sacrificing in any way the organization of the content of education, in that which relates to the fundamental themes of a society in reconstruction, the participation of the learners in defining content has indisputable significance. It is also their right, as active participants, to have a voice in the definition of what they need to know in order the better to serve the collective good.

Thus, in addressing what needs to be known in Guinea-Bissau at the basic level of literacy and post-literacy education, we focus also on the issue of a "mass line." We focus, that is, on the line which, when mobilized, the masses take from the beginning of the process of their formation. They are the active Subjects in this process.

In this sense, literacy and post-literacy education is, from the beginning, a working with the masses and not on them.

In schools like the Democratic Center, active learners and not the privileged take part in the organization of the program of study. This ensures that the fundamental objectives of the plan for the society will never be sacrificed. The same should be true in the literacy and post-literacy education of adults. The concretization of these objectives demands clarity about the relationship between production and education of which literacy and post-literacy are but one aspect.

This relationship becomes apparent as the overall plan for the society is defined. Why is anything produced? What should be produced? How should it be produced? These questions have repercussions in the form of social relations within production and the role played by the worker, as well as in the question of who benefits from production.

In a capitalist perspective the various factors in production—means of production on the one hand, workers on the other—combine in the service of capital. Part of the accumulated profits, which are not paid to the worker who sells his labor to the capitalist, are used for the capitalist's own well-being. Another part is used to buy more labor and more means of production which, together, produce more goods to be sold. The capitalist is interested in the production of goods—not, however, in terms of their usefulness but rather in their value as a means of exchange, that is, goods that can be sold. What is more, he seeks to produce "goods whose value covers and surpasses the sum of the values of his investment in production—the means of production and the labor."[3]

What workers receive as salary for their effort expended in the act of production corresponds only minimally to their effort. What is available for their living is also minimal and, therefore, the wage-earner class reproduces itself.

Deprived of the product of his labor, the worker has no say in the determination of what will be produced. To the degree that a significant quantity of what is produced does not correspond with the real needs of individuals, it is necessary to invent new needs. Thus a society becomes totally ambiguous when, while attempting to follow socialism, it allows itself to become fascinated by the myth of consumerism. If it moves in this direction, even though it does not have a capitalist class, its objective will be to produce goods to be sold. Socialism, in its very being, is something quite different from "a capitalist society without capitalists."[4]

"Buy what you already have" may be a caricature but it is one way to describe a capitalist society, a society of consumption. The role advertising plays in this society—in which the alienation of conscience is constantly increasing—is, indeed, fundamental. We do not need advertising to convince us to buy beans or rice, but we do need advertising to purchase this or that brand of perfume and even to buy this or that kind of rice—even if the difference is only in the packaging.

If production is governed by the well-being of the total society, rather than by the capitalist, private or state, then the accumulation of capital—indispensable to development—has a totally different significance and goal. The part of the accumulated capital that is not paid to the worker is not taken from him but is his quota toward the development of the collectivity. And what is to be produced with this quota are not goods defined as necessarily salable but goods that are socially necessary. For this it is essential that a society reconstruct itself in a revolutionary manner if it intends to become a society of workers whose leadership renounces both the tendency to leave everything to chance and the hardening of bureaucracy.

In a society that is capitalist, and therefore class-conscious as well as without political consciousness, the workers are better off, from the point of view of the dominant class. In a revolutionary society that looks toward socialism, on the other hand, the greater the political consciousness of individuals with regard to the re-creation of the society as it moves toward becoming a society of workers, the more wholeheartedly they give themselves to productive efforts. Their political consciousness is a factor in their attitude toward production. In a capitalist society, the education of workers has as one of its goals the continuation of a class of wage earners, obliged to sell their labor to the capitalist class. The education required to continue reproducing this class is one that will continuously increase the efficiency of the workers in their participation in the work process.* This process, as Marx points out, is one involving "objects bought by the capitalist, objects that belong to him": labor, on the one hand; the means of production on the other.[5]

The more lucratively these are combined in the production of things that have a high exchange value—marketable commodities—the better. Education in the service of this lucrative combination obviously cannot have as its objective to reveal the alienating character of the process. What it must do, therefore, is to hide it, reducing education to the mere transference of know-how, seen as neutral.

This is only one of the important aspects of the relation between education and production in capitalist society.

In the society seeking to reconstruct itself along socialist lines, on the contrary, basing itself on the new material reality which is taking shape, education should be preeminently revealing and critical.

In this sense, it is just as contradictory that such a society be oriented toward consumerism or rigid bureaucracy as it would be contradictory that an authoritarian and prescriptive educational system come into being, born of that same bureaucratic rigidity. Such a system has no place for the incorporation of militant learners and teachers in the authentic sense defined by Samora Machel.

At this point, in what may appear to be a digression, I would

---

*With this comment I do not mean to suggest that the education of workers in capitalist societies is designed to give the worker an overall understanding of the production process. Such an understanding is hardly indispensable to the capitalist system. Quite the contrary! "The more science is incorporated into the labor process, the less the worker understands of the process; the more sophisticated an intellectual product the machine becomes, the less control and comprehension of the machine the worker has. In other words, the more the worker needs to know in order to remain a human being at work, the less does he or she know. This is the chasm which the notion of 'average skill' conceals" (Harry Braverman, *Labor and Monopoly Capital: The Degradation of Work in the Twentieth Century* [London and New York: Monthly Review Press, 1974], p. 425).

like to comment on the Brazilian experience in adult literacy before the coup of 1964 and on the Chilean experience under the Christian Democratic government and under the Popular Unity leadership. Perhaps through just a few comments we can clarify some of the points we are addressing in this letter.

The Brazilian experience took place under the aegis of a populist regime. Here we were able to take advantage both of the free spaces it offered and also of the strong motivation for literacy of the urban masses and, in some areas, of the rural people. In rural areas, this motivation occurred principally in places where the people were engaged, with some conflict, in attempting to repossess the land or in struggling for better pay. The Peasant Leagues, especially in the northeast of Brazil, are an example of the results of the agitation of the peasants and of their spirit of organization. It is very important to say, however, that it was not any literacy campaign for adults that gave rise to the Peasant Leagues. Nor did they come into being with the ability to carry on the struggle which they developed later. The peasants initially came together to seek solutions to vital problems, among them that of the proper burial of their dead. That experience, without a doubt, led them to modes of action that were increasingly political, and brought about their engagement later in the struggle for repossession of the land and better salaries. It was this, in the end, that gave meaning to literacy. Some kind of radical experience appears, thus, to be necessary for the struggle itself, even though no alteration may have taken place in the social relations of production due to this experience. For many, literacy was seen in this situation as one more tool for bringing about the transformation of relations.

The two great workers' strikes in the rural areas of Pernambuco in 1961, the first with 83,000 workers and the second with 230,000 strikers, are clear examples of this phenomenon.

Thus the tone of the literacy campaign in Brazil was eminently political. It was to our interest in the historical situation in which we found ourselves to establish as close a link as possible between the literacy education and the political consciousness of the masses. Thus in the context of the Brazilian experience, the relationship between the literacy education of adults and production was expressed in criticism of the means of capitalist production characteristic of the country as a whole until today. Especially is this true of the urban centers and in the critical analysis of social relations in production in the rural areas.

For obvious reasons, it was not in our thinking to relate literacy education for adults to production simply in terms of technical training for the illiterates.

It was for this reason also that the Brazilian campaign, without giving up its national character, established certain priorities. Between acting in an area where popular consciousness was still buried and in one where popular rebellion was visible, we did not hesitate in choosing the second.

In the case of Chile, the literacy campaign took place in two distinct periods. In the first instance, it took place within the framework of the reformist bourgeois Christian Democrats; in the second, during the government of the Popular Unity Party, which looked toward the creation of a socialist society.

In both cases in Chile literacy was associated with production and the technical qualifications of the workers, but the political vision of the two regimes were diametrically opposed.

We might say that in the Brazilian case the motivation for literacy among the masses was related to the desire for change, even though the vision of what was involved was vague and imprecise.

In Chile, in the first stage (during the Christian Democratic government), motivation toward literacy was related to deepening the reforms already realized, such as agrarian reform. This, in its turn, gave adult literacy education a functional role. In the period of Popular Unity, the quality was increased and the role was expanded.

Very frequently Chilean peasants, as they conversed with me or as they spoke in the Culture Circles, noted the very concrete reasons that had led them to seek literacy education. They insisted that prior to the agrarian reform they had no reason to learn to read and to write, even when their "patron was understanding" and made it possible, because they "had no way to use their letters."

The case of Guinea-Bissau is different but also problematical. Indisputably, the war of liberation, as a "cultural fact and a factor of culture" (Amilcar Cabral), became a sort of midwife for the popular consciousness. It was not mere happenstance that, in the Culture Circle that Elza and I visited, the comrades said, "The struggle today is the same as yesterday, with some differences. Yesterday, with weapons in our hands, we sought to expel the invader. Today, still vigilant, with weapons in our hands, we pursue the struggle of production for the reconstruction of our country."

I also remember that in the same meeting another comrade said to me that the struggle for production—which should be the result of the work of everyone—requires total commitment to the collective interest, which should always be more important than individual interests.

Let us suppose that, growing out of the struggle for liberation, the political consciousness of the great majority of the population corresponds to the level of clarity of the comments I have just cited. There remains, nevertheless, a problem we must think about, in the area of the relationship between education and production. The problem is basic. It has to do not only with the organization of the programmatic content of literacy and post-literacy, to confine ourselves to this field, but also with the very validity of the struggle for literacy.

I refer to the fact that alterations in the social relations of production in the country have already occurred and are still occurring. These are alterations that will necessarily add a new dimension to the learning of reading and writing and to the continuity of this learning as it broadens and deepens.

In Brazil, as I said before, literacy education in rural areas, even without the alterations having occurred, made sense only to those within the peasant population who were involved in situations of conflict and who saw within them one more tool for their struggle. This is not the situation in Guinea-Bissau, where, in the war of liberation, people have what no literacy campaign could ever have offered them.

In Guinea-Bissau today, literacy and post-literacy education for adults are clearly political. They need a material point of reference within the transformation that is taking place, capable of giving them visibility in the eyes of the great majority within the country. In other words, it is necessary that the majority perceives a real need to read and write, which would not have existed if the concrete context had continued to function traditionally. This was true even in the "older liberated areas," where the population was directly involved in the struggle for liberation, participating in the effort to produce enough so that they could guarantee food for the troops. In the educational work realized by the PAIGC, an identical problem is posed.

It is one thing to link adult literacy and post-literacy to production in an area where the social relations of production are beginning to change in the direction of socialist production, and where cooperatives are created, from bottom to top, with this spirit. It is quite another thing to attempt the same relationship where there is no change in material conditions.

In the first case, literacy and post-literacy are responding to a real need. As the context changes, and things get better, the tendency is to become increasingly dynamic. This on the one hand changes, although not necessarily automatically, the way individuals perceive their reality; and, on the other, it results in the widening of their horizons. They become more curious about other parts of their world. Thus, many things that made no sense in the traditional context, because they were not functional, are important in the context of transformation. In these circumstances the chance of regressive illiteracy is limited to a normal minimum.

In the second case, where conditions for change do not exist, the possibility of failure accompanies the literacy struggle from the beginning; the chances of regressive illiteracy are enormous.

This is not pure opinion, but a statement of the facts as they are being verified in very different experiments in literacy education of adults wherever these are taking place.

It is for this reason that it appears to us that a campaign of adult literacy in Guinea-Bissau, even if it is national in scope, ought to begin\* in the areas where the process of transformation is underway, and, possibly, in those places where, following the plan of the government and of the Party, certain changes will take place within a short time. In this hypothesis, literacy education could even stimulate some of the changes.

It is possible to see, once again, the importance of the interdepartmental commission that Comrade Mario Cabral intends to create; closely related to the government and the Party, it will outline the general shape of the policies that will be followed in the literacy campaign.

To begin the campaign only in those areas whose material conditions are beginning to improve does not negate the national character of the campaign; it assures its results.

Without losing the vision of the total plan for the society, the local conditions of the area where work is begun must be kept in mind when the definition of what needs to be known is made; that is, in the organization of the programmatic content of literacy and post-literacy education. It is on the basis of these local conditions that the more general situation is understood. Thus, every generative word ought to make possible an analysis which, starting with the local, is then naturally extended to the regional, national, continental and, finally, to the universal.

This same methodological principle applies equally to post-literacy education.

Simply to offer an example, we might take the generative word "rice," whose significance for Guinea-Bissau is indisputable, and see how, starting with the rich theme to which it refers, it is possible to organize most of the programmatic content, not only for the literacy education of adults, but for post-literacy, primary and even secondary levels.

The team attempting such an undertaking would be attentive to the general political principles of the Party and the government—the social plan that determines what needs to be known, how, why, and in whose benefit, as well as what needs to be produced, how, for what and for whom.

Without giving attention to all of the thematic areas as-

---

\*When I say "begin" I am referring to the work to be developed by FARP realized within the armed forces and to which is linked what is going on in certain urban sections of Bissau.

sociated with the word rice, nor to the rigorous ordering of sequence, I shall indicate some of them which, necessarily, are related to many others not suggested here.

The theme of each of the learning or knowledge units that I shall present are simply examples. They will be arranged differently and much more completely when they are studied by a national interdisciplinary team. They will also be enriched by nuances we cannot imagine when they become a topic for debate among the learners; in this way the learners make their contribution to the organization of the programmatic content of their own education.

As an introduction to the study of the different program units, related to each other around the theme "rice," it is possible to analyze the relationship between human beings and nature. Always we take as a point of reference the concrete reality of the learners and their own experience in this reality.

Such an analysis involves clarifying a series of important points. I shall make reference to only a few. Work is one of these. The analysis of work starts not with the idea of work but with the concrete reality of the work in which the individuals are engaged.

"Work is, in the first place, a process of interaction between nature and man, a process in which man realizes, regulates, and controls, by means of his own action, his material interaction with nature."[6]

The discussion about work, then, opens up the possibility of debate about culture, which in itself constitutes one of the most important units of study: culture and national identity; the positive and negative aspects of this culture; the necessity to overcome the negative aspects of culture, which Cabral used to call the "weaknesses of culture"; culture and the production of rice; culture and health; culture and food; poetry, sculpture in wood, the dance; cultural invasion; cultural alienation.

On the other hand, the analysis of work also makes possible the study of the processes of work and its social organization, the study of different modes of productions: precapitalist, capitalist, socialist.

All of this can be done in a simple way—by which I mean neither simplistic nor sophisticated.

I would like, at this stage, to underline several points. First, that this is an introductory theme does not in any way mean that it will not also be present in the discussions of the units that follow. Second, in the discussion, which implies the preparation of a wide variety of audio-visual materials, no concession should be made to violent and disruptive oratory by participants.

Finally, it appears to me important to underline that the position, not always explicit, which holds that such a theme is "too theoretical and thus not interesting to workers and rural peasants, and, thus, not even understood by them" is based on a false vision of the theory and is eminently elitist.

Amilcar Cabral, in seminars for the training of activists, analyzed themes of great practical and theoretical relevance in a truly concrete and objective way. He never minimized the capacity of his peasant comrades to understand. Amilcar affirmed that the middle-class intellectual needed the courage to commit class suicide before being reborn as a revolutionary worker, able to contribute to the struggle for liberation. For him, this was neither a cliche nor a rhetorical play on words.

Amilcar Cabral spoke of what he had done. He never saw himself as an exclusive possessor of truth and of revolutionary knowledge that he ought, as a momentary gesture of altruism, to offer as a present to his peasant colleagues. On the contrary, like every true revolutionary Cabral was always a teacher learning from his people, from whom they, for this very reason, were constantly learning.

His analyses of "the role of the peasant," of the "unity in the struggle," and of "reality," to cite only a few, are examples of what I have just affirmed.

My experience, now a long while ago, in Recife was quite different. It began not so much in the field of literacy as of post-literacy, and, in an apparent paradox, paid little attention to whether the participants in the Culture Circles were literate or not.

In the beginning of my work, my surprise in the face of the critical positions assumed by these unschooled workers arose from the perception that I had up to that time that these were positions held exclusively by university students. My surprise had its origin in my own class position, increased by my university training—perhaps, to be more accurate, I should say by my elitist university training.

It was as a result of those first experiences that I became dedicated to adult literacy. And after that I never hesitated to propose a unit on the critical understanding of culture as part of the introduction to the study of reading and writing.

Let us see now some of the possible unit themes interrelated around the word rice: production of rice, geography of rice, history of rice, health and rice.

### Production of rice:

The production of rice in Guinea-Bissau, beginning with the analysis of this in the geographical area where work is going on in literacy and post-literacy. The social relations of production. Agricultural techniques or planting and harvesting rice in both wet and dry regions. Preparation of areas to be cultivated. Traditional techniques; modern techniques. Plant pathologies. The cultural outlook of different ethnic groups, their work instruments and techniques. A comparative analysis of rice culture with other cultures necessary for the reconstruction of the country; peanuts, wheat, sweet potatoes, mandioca, cashew. Agriculture and industry. Production and distribution of agricultural products. Acres planted and production per acre; measures necessary to increase the number of acres cultivated and to intensify the production per acre. The role of rice in the general economy of the country. The internal distribution of rice and its external commercial potential. The factors in external trade. Division and reconstruction of the country. National defense interests. Cooperatives for the production of rice, etc.

### Geography:

The geographical areas for the cultivation of rice in Guinea-Bissau, beginning, of course, with the area where the literacy work is taking place. The international geography of rice cultivation.

### Politics:
The political plan of the government and beginning with reference to the cultivation of rice, and moving to production in general. National defense interests.

### History:
Rice in Guinea-Bissau. Rice in other regions of the world.

### Health:
Rice, nutrition and health. Health and work. Health and education. Health, work, education and national reconstruction.

Before ending this, I would like to make a few additional comments. I know very well that the realization of certain aspects of the dynamics of a scheme such as this raises a series of problems.

The first aspect I want to emphasize is the opportunity offered, for example, through the study of the geography of rice, also to study the geography of Guinea-Bissau; through the study of the history of rice, also to study the history of the country, the history of the first resistance to the invader, the history of the liberation struggle, the history being made today through the reconstruction of the country in the interest of the creation of a new society.

And finally, through this study of Guinea-Bissau, in its most varied and interrelated aspects, one becomes aware of the African situation and of this in terms of the world.

Another important aspect is the active role that the participants in the Culture Circles must play from the beginning of the discussions, including the pre-program presentation as a work project. Individuals and groups should have, if the project is accepted, an active role in the collection of local data, basic to various parts of the program. All kinds of data must be assembled locally—about the area of rice cultivation, the way this cultivation takes place, the number of cultivatable acres and the number actually under cultivation, the difficulties the peasants meet in their daily work, the number of inhabitants of the area, distribution, the means of communication, work instruments, health, education, etc.

This investigative activity is itself highly educational, and also increases the information of the educators or offers them entirely new information. What is more, the results offer a source of information of inestimable value to the government. The peasants in Chile carried out projects like this, making a socio-cultural diagnosis of their communities and even being responsible for the tabulation of the data.

The outline I have suggested as an example revolved around the world "rice." It could equally well have been related to the word "wheat," or "peanuts," or some other word.

During the early phases of literacy education, analyses of the themes that grow out of the generative words are closely linked to concrete realities in local, regional and national settings, and are necessarily at an introductory level. The process of deepening that level takes place during the post-literacy education phase. In this sense, the post-literacy phase is continuous with what began earlier. It is part of a deepening and diversification process, part of the same act of knowing begun during the first stages of literacy education.

Putting any such plan into practice, it must be emphasized, raises problems about the organization (as decentralized as possible), the training of teacher-educators, and the preparation of the necessary teaching materials.

In reality, moreover, to the degree that we seek even minimal efficiency in establishing relations between production and literacy and post-literacy, we must understand that the challenges we will confront are many and varied. They are not always easily answered. The training of active educators is one of those challenges. Educators who enter into dialogue with active learners find that the process is mediated by the concrete reality which, together, they and the learners must know and transform.

As a whole, the relation between literacy and post-literacy, production and education, involves two levels, inextricably interwoven. The first level is an understanding of the process of production itself—what, how, for what and for whom to produce. The second level is the introduction of new techniques which require new tools and their use.

If we consider just these two points, which in themselves obviously do not exhaust the universe of the training of activist educators, we can see how serious and complex is the challenge we all have. It is important that in replying to the challenge, conscious of its seriousness and complexity, we do not give in to the temptation of perfectionism.

We must do what we can today with whatever small resources we have. Only in this way will it be possible to do tomorrow what we could not do today.

*With a fraternal embrace,*
*Paulo Freire*

# Letter 12

Geneva
February 3, 1976

Engineer Mario Cabral
State Commissioner for Education and Culture
Bissau, Guinea-Bissau

*Comrade Mario,*
You should by now have received Miguel's letter regarding our next visit.

It gives me great satisfaction to send you a copy of the latest letter to the team, addressed to Comrade Monica and in response to one that she wrote me, which caught us up on a series of activities of great significance in the literacy and post-literacy work of FARP.

We learned through Monica of the creation of the National

Commission, which we should probably meet while we are there.

I believe it would be essential for us to talk with the Commission about several aspects, at least, of the general problem of literacy and post-literacy and their necessary connections with the educational system of the country, as well as the relation of education with the overall plan for the society which you are seeking to create. Some of these aspects were referred to in my last letter of which you also received a copy.

I am eager to be there with all of you and send my fraternal embrace.

*Paulo Freire*

# Letter 13

Geneva
February 3, 1976

*Comrade Teresa Monica,*

I have just received your letter. I hasten to write you even though we are on the eve of our next visit to Guinea. Then, I hope, we will be able to discuss more thoroughly with the team the matters you have referred to.

Today let me offer only a few first reactions to the central aspects of your letter.

The first of these has to do with post-literacy education. I wrote about this at some length in my last letter in which I tried to emphasize that it is a continuation, deepened and diversified, of the same act of knowing that is initiated in literacy education.

You seem, from your letter, to be achieving something very interesting in post-literacy work which, even from your critical vantage point, seems good although that does not seem to you to be true of all that you are doing.

Your notion of a basic book for the coordinators in the training seminars for post-literacy seems to me a really good idea.

I understand that you would plan to add to the different texts some considerations or analyses in the field of beginning scientific language "at a level which is perfectly accessible to the majority of the learners" who have completed the first phase of their learning.

I would like to make two comments about this proposal. I must insist that the first of these comments is in no way a criticism of your project. In making it, it is simply as though I were thinking out loud. The second is a question which contains a suggestion.

When, in referring to the book for coordinators, you say, "For each text, we would seek grammatical and scientific content at the fourth-grade level . . .," I am fearful lest the team may be affected by the concept of the traditional primary school—which is necessary to provide entrance to secondary school, which, in its turn, is seen as an introduction to university level, which at the moment does not exist in Guinea-Bissau.

My comment may have nothing to do with the intention of the team but it seems to me worth talking about. Once again, we see how it is not possible to think of literacy and post-literacy apart from the whole educational system and how, through concrete and realistic measures, it is as indispensable as it is urgent that this be reformulated. In another part of your letter you refer to this relation between literacy, post-literacy and the educational system when you speak of the question of teaching Portuguese and Creole.

In an attempt to clarify my fear, which takes me back to my last letter, I would say we should avoid from the beginning establishing any type of formal—or, worse yet, legal—equivalence between the program content of literacy and post-literacy and the different grade levels of the traditional school. This is especially true since the traditional schools will be replaced as soon as possible by a new model more compatible with the overall plan for the society.*

---

*This does not mean that later as the new educational system takes form, it will be impossible to establish equivalencies between post-literacy training and the various levels of Basic Instruction.

Actually the most important thing is that the learner in a literacy class become engaged in an act of knowing that will continue to deepen and become diversified. One should not have to have before one the myth of a secondary school to which one will be promoted only if one satisfies primary-school requirements during literacy and post-literacy classes. So it is important that the new educational system, which will emerge from the social practice of the country, is not in any sense a pyramid, a whole composed of parts whose function it is to select learners to be sent on to some later stage of education.

Thus primary education, while it is still the responsibility of the total system and maintains relations with the rest of the parts, is not seen as a "path" leading to a higher point. In discussing the educational system that serves the Tanzanian social plan, President Nyerere, in his excellent work "Education for Self-Reliance," said, "The education offered in our primary schools should be an education complete in itself. It should not continue to be simply a preparation for secondary school. Instead of the activities of the primary school being aimed at competitive examinations which select the few who will go to secondary school, they should constitute preparation for the life which the majority of children will lead."[7]

It might be interesting to clarify that for Nyerere "preparation for life" does not have the same naive meaning that it has for so many, according to which the school, outside of life, would serve as the center of preparation for life, a kind of parenthesis during which we are prepared to enter life. This was the concept attacked by Dewey, for whom the school had to be life itself and not preparation for it.

For Nyerere, preparation for life consists of a critical understanding of the life actually lived; only thus is it possible to create new ways of living. His thought, which is both pedagogical and political, is nourished by what is real, concrete, and based on experience, the transformation of which is the central educational activity.

I do not know if I have been sufficiently consistent in this comment which, let me say again, does not imply a negative criticism of the book project to which you referred.

The second comment takes me to another topic in your letter where you spoke of the "enormous quantity of writings, veritable historical works, done by the learners" which you "don't know the best way to make use of."

Emphasizing one of the topics already discussed, I would ask whether the preparation of the book for coordinators could not become an excellent opportunity to make use of at least some of the texts written by the learners. Inserting some of these learner texts in simple language into the books would be the task of the team. Following each text might be considerations of this or that aspect of the subject to which it refers.

But let us leave aside for the moment the book project for the coordinators, and look only at the written work produced by the learners. Would it not be possible now to take advantage of the dynamics you refer to that seem to be developing in each Culture Circle and also, through letters, between learners in different Circles? Could you not begin to exchange the texts? They could be read and discussed, and might lead to the preparation of still others in response to the challenges they contain.

On the other hand, before it might be possible to edit these for a complete book of these writings for different uses, you might consider in relation to what we have been talking about here, publishing them periodically in *Nô Pintcha,* as well as perhaps making use of them in a radio program planned for this purpose.

In whatever different ways you find to use this material, it seems to me that the creative power of the people should be emphasized. This creative power is indispensable to the reconstruction of the country.

You have also given a good many very interesting examples of what we might consider to be attempts at post-literacy, about which I said so much in my last letter.

The reading and discussion of themes, proposed by the Bissau newspaper, written and oral work related to important national dates or to events in the liberation struggle growing out of the military experience of members of the Circles are some of these examples. To them I would add the discussion around

the theme "factory" along the same lines that I suggested with
relation to "rice," in response to which you remarked that
"many very profound matters have come out of what was
touched on by the learners."

Your critical reflection on your daily experience with the
learners and coordinators will, more than anything else, help
you find ways to fill the "certain gaps" that you say exist in your
work at its present stage. This critical reflection on your praxis
is absolutely indispensable. It should never be confused with
meaningless alienating and alienated talk. While it is the source
of knowledge, praxis is not, however, a theory in itself. It is only
when we give ourselves constantly to critical reflection on it that
praxis makes possible the development of theory, which, in its
turn, illumines new practice.

I keep insisting that my letters are not prescriptive; they are,
rather, challenges to you and to myself, made so that we may
come to reflect more deeply on the praxis of a project that is
going on—a project that does not in all of its aspects repeat the
experience of projects in which I have participated previously.

The fundamental problem confronting you—one of the
"gaps" that you mentioned—is how to integrate various aspects
of the reconstruction of the country into post-literacy work. The
central question posed is that the reconstruction of the country
cannot be reduced to a simple object of knowledge for our
curiosity. How, for example, can we attempt to understand a
plow in its different parts, in its mechanism, in its use? Reconstruction requires a variety of knowledge at different levels, in
different areas, interrelated in themselves and in direct relation
to the overall plan for the society. It cannot be something we
speak of in the past but must be, rather, something we know in
the process of doing it. From this comes the necessity to relate
education in general to the production process, which is the
source of that variety of knowledge necessary for the dynamism
that should characterize the struggle for reconstruction.

In the letter that Miguel just sent to Comrade Mario Cabral
about our next visit we looked forward to as far-ranging a conversation as possible on this subject.

Another subject you spoke of in your letter, which must be

taken up again during our visit as you suggest, is that of what language should be the basis of literacy work.

In truth, the process of liberation of a people does not take place in profound and authentic terms unless this people reconquers its own Word, the right to speak it, to "pronounce" it, and to "name" the word: to speak the word as a means of liberating their own language through that act from the supremacy of the dominant language of the colonizer.

The imposition of the language of the colonizer on the colonized is a fundamental condition of colonial domination which also is extended to neocolonial domination. It is not by chance that the colonizers speak of their own language as "language" and the language of the colonized as "dialect"; the superiority and richness of the former is placed over against the poverty and inferiority of the latter.

Only the colonizers "have a history," since the history of the colonized is presumed to have begun with the civilizing presence of the colonizers. Only the colonizers "have" culture, art and language and are civilized national citizens of the world which "saves" others. The colonized lacked a history before the "blessed" efforts of the colonizers. The colonized are uncultured and "barbarian natives."

Without the right of self-definition, they are given a profile by the colonizers.[9] They cannot, for this reason, "name themselves" nor "name" the world of which they have been robbed.

In one of the writings in which he discusses the role of culture in the liberation struggle, Amilcar Cabral makes some analyses which apply to the problem of language. This analysis takes place precisely when he speaks of the assimilation—de-Africanization—of the urban minorities; they, living under and surrounded by the colonial power, give themselves to the culture and to the dominant language; in contrast is the vast majority of the peasant population, who escape the more destructive power of the colonizers and survive, preserving significant traces of their culture.

In a certain sense, these de-Africanized urban minorities take on a strange sort of bicultural character,[9] an expression of their cultural alienation, which is something not quite the same as being bilingual. The more alienated these urban minorities are, the more they struggle to deny their own roots; they forget or never learn their own language, defined by the colonizer as a dialect, something poor and inferior. In this way, "nostalgically" attracted by the dominant culture which gives them an inferior profile, in the denial of their culture they deny their own being. It is for this reason that Amilcar Cabral insisted on the need for the re-Africanization of those intellectuals who would give themselves to the cause of liberation.

The rural people succeeded in remaining immune to this strange biculturism. Fortified by their own cultural richness, which even Amilcar Cabral included in what he used to call "weakness of culture," they preserved their language. They not only communicated in this language but also defended themselves from the aggressive alienation of the colonizers.

As a society overcomes its state of colonial dependence, attempting to remake itself in a revolutionary manner, as in Guinea-Bissau, it cannot really escape the stabilizing of its linguistic problem. The problem was actually posed for the society in the liberation struggle.

Thus the urgency, in the case of Creole, that it be affirmed as the national language—just as was true of Portuguese with reference to Latin. This will involve a serious effort to give it rules and a system as a written language, since as a spoken language it already has its own structure.

The role which you underline in your letter that Creole has been playing in national unity, ever since the hard days of the struggle, appears indisputable. I would not hesitate to place the work of "regulating" it as a written language, which obviously demands the orientation of competent linguists, among the priorities of the struggle for reconstruction of the country.

I share, thus, the uncertainties that result, above all, from your praxis. With a brotherly embrace,

*Paulo Freire*

# Letter 14

Geneva
April 1976

Engineer Mario Cabral
Commissioner of State for Education and Culture
Bissau, Republic of Guinea-Bissau

*Comrade Mario Cabral,*
    I am sending you several copies of the letter I have just written to the Literacy Commission. One is for you and the others are for other comrades whom you feel might be interested in its contents.

One of my fundamental intentions every time I write a letter, whether long or short, is to provoke—in myself as I write and in the comrades as they read—critical reflection on the concrete problems that we confront in the fascinating process of national reconstruction.

Whenever I speak of projects in which Elza and I have been involved at some time in the past, I find myself re-living events that had for us the same intensity as the problems we know now in "our" Guinea-Bissau. My intention is always the same, that of inviting the comrades to whom I write to assume a critical posture that could result in re-creating, within a specific situation, the situation described by my pen.

It is never my intention, however, to suggest that each letter of mine should be some A-B-C, a finished formula for you. Not only would such an attitude espress disrespect for the integrity of the comrades, it would also be a demonstration that I had not understood one of your greatest characteristics, that is, the harmony you have achieved between true humility that allows you to accept the contribution of a foreigner as appropriate to the interests of the country and your profound sense of autonomy which cannot be wounded. These virtues which express your political maturity are not learned in seminars nor are they made in laboratories. PAIGC, in its turn, did not invent them. They were truly forged in the praxis of liberation in which the oppressed people of Guinea became the great teacher-learner of their leaders. Amilcar Cabral is the perfect symbol of these virtues.

It was exactly this spirit of self-respect, of vigilance, of care with history, which as it is being made by you is at the same time being remade, that moved all of us at IDAC to this almost unrestrained desire to offer the best of ourselves to your struggle for the reconstruction of Guinea-Bissau and the Cape Verde Islands. While it is the best of ourselves, we recognize it to be very little, considering the limits of each one.

Perhaps it would be possible to say, putting humility aside, that one of the best methods of reading my letters would be, after trying to understand their overall meaning, to try to extract from them possible lines of work that I may not have perceived but which may be found hidden in one or another affirmation within the body of the letter. In essence, to read a letter deeply is to rewrite it.

I have not been too well lately, which has led me to have to curtail my commitments a bit. There is no doubt, however, that I will soon be there again, when I hope to have a solemn meeting with the mangoes and cashews. What nostalgia I have for them!

Elza and I intend to stay a few days beyond the week officially programmed for our visit for some extra activity. One activity will be with the Literacy Commission (not the national one), with Monica, Edna, Alvarenga, Paulo and José. It would be possible to organize other activities for us which might arise.

An embrace for you, for Comrade Beatriz, and affectionate greetings for your dear grandson Pansau (this time I think I have the spelling correct).

*Paulo*


An impertinent P.S.—
Dear Comrade Mario,

Although I have no news from there, I am hoping that the Commission re-created by you in the February synthesis meeting is indeed functioning with Edna, Monica, Alvarenga, Paulo and José. I don't know if there are others involved. You may remember that I wrote to this Commission, with copies to you.

The role of this Commission seems to me fundamentally important. The dynamism of the work in the civilian area will depend very much on what it is possible to do in the heart of this Commission. The Commission, in its turn, should furnish material to the National Commission, whose responsibility is to think through the general lines of the policies of the campaign. I made a similar request to Comrade Julinho in relation to FARP.

I hope you will forgive this insistence. It is the insistence of a comrade.

*Paulo*

# Letter 15

Geneva
April, 1976

*Comrades Monica, Edna, Alvarenga, Paulo and José,*

This is the first that I write to you in an explicit, almost official manner, addressing myself to the Commission, which I hope is not only in being but in full activity and composed of representatives of different interests in the literacy field, working, however, within the same lines that orient the politics of PAIGC and of the government.

In September of last year toward the end of our first visit, we took part in what we called the synthesis meeting, coordinated by Comrade Mario Cabral and attended by various departments of the Commission on Education and the team of IDAC. Among the many concrete and viable actions that today form the central nucleus of our collaborative program was the creation of two commissions. It was anticipated that the commissions, in turn, might create whatever other commissions, sub-commissions or committees that experience might require.

The first of these commissions was to be composed, at least in the beginning, of persons active at the grass roots. It would include those responsible for the progress of the Culture Circles for literacy and post-literacy in a specific sector, FARP, for example, and representatives of the civilian activity with ongoing projects—projects linked to the political committees of the neighborhoods, to youth, to women, etc.

The essential role of these commissions was, initially, to assure a certain standard of action among the different sectors of the work. They would also provide their members with an excellent opportunity, as they discussed their specific experiences, to learn from each other—from their strong points as well as their mistakes growing out of actual practice.

Basically, the meetings of this commission would be chiefly for evaluation in the sense I spoke about this process in earlier letters. They would also be concerned about programming. In this sort of evaluation members would look together at the practice completed or taking place in relation to certain objectives, above all the political objectives, that illumine present practice, in order to be more effective in the future.

It is for this reason that in meetings of active comrades nothing can be hidden, neither the things that have gone well nor the mistakes. It is in hiding these things that the real error lies.

In the fantastic effort that we are all engaged in Guinea-Bissau and the Cape Verde Islands, the challenge is not that we become individual specialists but that we discover with increasing clarity what we can actually do as a team.

We must not allow ourselves to use our success as a means of covering, discreetly or not, our weaknesses, or be tempted to place the blame for our weakness on nonexistent factors. As comrades committed to the same struggle, with the same objectives, we must learn what is obvious: no one knows everything; no one is ignorant of everything. The road, therefore, to overcoming our weaknesses lies not in hiding them, but in discussing them in concrete terms exactly where they are to be found.

In the same way, the road to reinforcing our strengths does not lie in keeping them for ourselves.

Finally, the efforts of this Commission will correct and improve practice as it develops locally. It will become an important support for the work of the National Commission as it plans the general policy growing out of what is happening locally and regionally. Comrades Mario Cabral and Julio Carvalho will always know what the Commission is doing and, when possible, will participate in its meetings.

I should like to return in this letter to a work proposal that I made six years ago to a group of Latin American educators in Mexico; in doing so, I shall be touching on certain points made already in these letters to you.

It will not be my intention to look on the proposal as a project, even though I may speak of it as a project in the course of the letter. I shall not, therefore, be following the normal procedure for presenting a project—analyzing the different stages in detail, including an estimated budget. That can all be done later when we have seen whether the suggestions themselves have any relevance for this country and whether they fit the immediate objectives of the Party and the government. In short, we must see whether they have any viability in the light of present conditions in the country.

Before describing the proposal, I want to say a bit about the roots from which it came. When I was a child, I learned my first letters from my parents in the shade of a wonderful mango tree in the yard of the old house where I was born in Recife. The words that I first learned were the words of my child's universe. My first blackboard was the ground itself, and my first chalk a small stick.

Much later, in Chile, I had occasion to see words written by newly literate peasants with their farm implements on the roads leading to their work fields.

Both of these experiences, so distant in time and space from each other yet in other ways so closely related, suggested to me the thoughts presented years ago and now revived in this letter. Additional nuances will be added this time that were not present earlier.

The basic idea of the proposal is to select an agricultural area that is undergoing changes in its infrastructure—like those mentioned in Letter 11. Such change might come about due to the creation of a Culture Circle. The existential experience of the population as a whole would constitute the basic source from which the total educational undertaking would be drawn; in this case, agricultural production would be the central focus. This proposal would apply not only to literacy education for adults but to the education of children and adolescents also. While productive work would provide the concrete context, it would also provide the theoretical context within which to reflect on the practice of production. As far as possible there would be an attempt to comprehend the dynamic movement between practice and theory in the context of practice itself.

This means, on the one hand, that educational activity could take place in the fields—although not exclusively there—during the months of good weather and in some sort of simple shelter during the rainy season, at least until some more substantial building could be built. On the other hand, it means that education as an act both of knowledge and political activity, centered in a thematic derived from the concrete reality of the learners and closely associated with production, should be seen as an important factor in the process of transforming the thought of the people. Especially in the case of literacy education, the time dedicated to education should be seen as part of the day's work whenever that seems necessary. It is equally important as a form of productive work.

The first great "codification," the decoding of which reveals a series of components of the work process, is the natural formation of the area, extended, because of the transforming presence of human beings living there, to include the cultural formation.

As the whole village becomes a large Culture Circle with everyone engaged together in the educational process, all at the same time become both learners and teachers. From their work with the land—planting and harvesting—and in providing the minimal services necessary to care for local health, mutual assistance should receive maximum attention and its advantages over individualistic activities stressed.

In such a project, the informal educational experience, which is never strange or far away from any human community, is systematized without being bureaucratized.

There would be a place for a small band of educators, well prepared and willing to become completely incorporated into the life of the community. They would participate with the peasants in all of the productive activities and would, in addition, take on the task of systematizing the informal learning mentioned above. They would do it *with* the population, not *for* it.

The general boundary marking the programmatic content of education at whatever level (that is, the determination of what needs to be known as described in Letter 11) is really the existential experience of the people, taken as a whole, of which productive activity is the determining dimension.

What is being attempted in this kind of education is the exercise of critical reflection, at deeper and deeper levels, about how human beings live in their world. It means taking the daily routine itself as an object of analysis, trying to penetrate its meaning. It means replacing knowledge based largely on feelings about the facts by knowledge based on the underlying meaning, the *raison d'être*, of those facts.

This was what Amilcar Cabral tried to do when he used to turn the encampments of the liberation struggle into a place for theoretical debate. He considered it of the utmost importance to discuss with his militant comrades the progress of the struggle, the tactics to be used, the objectives to be achieved, as well as to debate the scientific explanation of thunder and lightning and the belief in the power of amulets.*Amilcar Cabral knew

---

*"Our new culture, whether inside or outside the school, must serve the resistance movement and the carrying out of the Party's program. It must be this way, my comrades. Our culture must be developed at the national level of our country. And this must be done without holding the culture of others in low esteem. We must take advantage of all of those things in the culture of others, of all that is good for us and of all that can be adapted to our conditions of life. Our culture must develop on the basis of science. It should be scientific, not based on a belief in imaginary things. Our culture should not allow any one of us to think that lightning is the result of God's anger or that thunder is a voice speaking from the skies or the fury of IRAN. Tomorrow everyone in our culture must know that thunder occurs when two clouds, carrying negative and positive

very well that all of these things were related to one another.

To the degree that the population begins to take its own daily experience—its own spontaneous way of being in the world—as the object of critical reflection, the programmatic content of education emerges in some of its most basic elements. The programmatic content structures itself around the different interrelated aspects that make up that spontaneous way of being in the world.

This spontaneous movement or orientation in the world implies more than merely existing. It means being *in* and *with* the world. It involves the self-awareness of the subjects who move and their consciousness of the world in which they move. It still does not necessarily imply that the world—reality—is truly known. Cabral insisted that "our culture must develop on a scientific base. We can no longer believe in imaginary things."

When persons are active Subjects of their own existence, their daily life is oriented toward reality. "From this base they form a kind of practical intution of reality in the midst of which they carry out their own lives of practical activity and feeling."[10]

The fundamental point, however, is that people not only see the world as the "base from which they carry out their own lives" but that they also see daily life as the object of an ever more rigorous knowledge. This knowledge should clarify and illuminate their practical and emotional existence that takes reality as its base. "The immediate, utilitarian practice," to cite Karel Kosik once again, "and the corresponding common sense that it engenders place humanity in a position to become oriented to the world, to become familiar with all the things that exist in it and to manage them, but they do not necessarily bestow the comprehension of the meaning of those things and of reality."[11] I would simply add to Kosik's comments that what is missing is a *critical comprehension* of things.

Militant educators and learners, when we are truly Subjects moving in the world, take on the role of Subjects who know the world that we are transforming and in which we move. It is our

---

electrical charges, bump into each other. First comes the lightning and then the noise which is thunder" (Amilcar Cabral, "Resistência cultural," in *PAIGC— Unidade e Luta*, pp. 198–99).

task, based on our critical analysis of our practice—that is, of all that we do—to achieve an ever more rigorous knowledge of reality as it is being transformed; we are both overcoming obstacles in daily life and clarifying it, including those ingenuous methods of confronting the concrete that Cabral calls "the weaknesses of culture."

It is in this connection that I insisted in Letter 11 that education always involves some theory of learning put in practice. This theory, in the perspective of PAIGC, demands that the learner assume an important role. According to this theory the learner has the critical role of one who also knows and not the passive attitude of a mere recipient of knowledge.

In a project such as I am suggesting, the militant educators also take part in productive work. Indeed, they become inhabitants of the area just as truly as those who live there. They should try to form study groups composed of around 15 or 20 persons who will discuss their daily experiences, debate matters related to their practical activities in behalf of production, and thus open up innumerable themes for analysis growing out of these debates.

The first step will be to mobilize the population and, in a general way, explain the project to them. From the mobilization comes the possibility of organization for the project. That, of course, is the moment when the educators can begin to comprehend the basic aspirations of the people and the vision they have of themselves and of the reality within their daily experience.

If, from the very first moment, the people are able to assume the project as their own and as significant for their lives, then they will be able to contribute to the general effort toward national reconstruction.

These, then, are the basic requirements. To the degree that they also coincide with the political principles of the Party and of the government, they will stimulate the creative, conscious participation of the people in the task of national reconstruction and in the creation of the new society. Without this popular participation, national reconstruction and the new society will not come into being.

There are two aspects of the project that affect the local population: the significance it has for the struggle to bring about national reconstruction, and its interpretation by the people. Its significance must be discussed clearly and objectively at the beginning and returned to as a theme during the whole process.

Without absolute care and precision about both of these aspects, the project could perish before it was actually born. If the people have not been committed to the struggle for national liberation, a phrase like "national reconstruction" could be extremely vague and abstract. For those who did participate in that struggle, it will have a concrete meaning. It is therefore necessary to plan, from the very first, in relation to local reality. Reconstruction must be so near and concrete that its meaning is clear—the reconstruction of the *barrio* or even of the street on which the people live. Having taken part in something concrete that they understand, the people can make the leap to regional or national issues. It is at the same time also necessary that projects like this be based on changes that have taken place or are about to take place in the structures that condition the lives of people. These changes in the traditional context of life create new expectations in the population and give to undertakings like literacy and post-literacy a meaning that makes them necessities of life. Thus a dynamism is established about the process of learning—at whatever level—that corresponds to the dynamism of the other changes taking place.

I do not know if you are familiar with the transformation in Tachai, a small mountain village in the north of China, which Dr. Lee considers "the most outstanding example of the application of literacy and ideological education of the masses for rural development."[12]

The case of Tachai, which has become a model for all of China and an attraction for educators from the whole world, clearly reveals the principle of dynamism to which I referred.

In 1945, after the expulsion of the Japanese troops by the Chinese Communist forces, "a plan was initiated for the beginning of a program of agrarian reform as a precondition for the development of the village." This project was linked to the motivation already existing as part of the experience of getting rid of the invader.

The first moment of the literacy campaign—preeminently

political in all of its phases—centered on discussions about agrarian reform.

The impetus to change local reality enabled the population to see the need for literacy by means of which they might better understand the need for reform. If the impetus for reform were lost, the movement toward literacy education would also disappear. Once agrarian reform was completed, the peasants perceived that they could not increase production (without which the transformation of Tachai would be frustrated) unless they had animals and work tools.

The experience of this new need, coming as part of the dynamic of transforming reality, brought a new phase in the literacy program which involved discussion about the advantages of organizing themselves for working together.

In this way, the felt need was critically perceived and the first response took the form of organizing a cooperative work team under the leadership of Chen Yung-kuei, who little by little had become the indisputable leader of development at Tachai.

The positive results achieved by Chen Yung-kuei and his comrades encouraged many other peasants, who then joined them. Thus, in 1952, the original team based on cooperative work became a simple cooperative. In 1956 it was recognized as a socialist cooperative, and in 1958 the village of Tachai became a "production brigade."

The process of popular education was integral to all of these changes, stimulating them and being stimulated by them.

Much later, after he had taken part as an illiterate in the literacy campaign in his village and léd the first cooperative work group, Chen, talking with a group of visiting American educators, summarized the reason for the transformation of his village: "It was the creative power of the people that changed Tachai and all of China."[13]

I would like to recapitulate rapidly, almost didactically, the basic steps in the Tachai experience showing the dynamic interaction between the structural changes and education—including literacy education for adults followed by a series of activities accomplished through study groups, to which I did not make reference in the remarks above:

a) During the Japanese occupation, there is exploitation, domination, and a failure of initiative among the people.

b) The expulsion of the invader in 1945 by the Chinese Communists awakens the opposite reaction in the people— hope, self-confidence—leading to a serious struggle to reconstruct the village.

c) The new climate created by liberation enables the people to become involved in a literacy campaign and in agrarian reform.

d) The campaign for learning to read and write leads to a deeper "reading" of their own reality, in which the socio-economic "readings" make clear the need for basic agrarian reforms.

e) Having perceived the urgency of reform, obstacles are perceived, and in this process a deeper political consciousness is formed.

f) The necessity for cooperative work emerges since only by combining forces can individual limitations in the productive process be overcome, production increased, and victories consolidated.

g) Education accompanies the movement from solitary work to cooperation, and the "production brigade" is established.

As a parenthesis within this discussion of work, I would like to return to the relation between education and the overall plan for the society.

A plan for a society like the one we have been discussing cannot be realized except on a very limited scale if, within the overall plan for that society, the established policy for economic development is oriented toward rapid industrialization to be accomplished by means of a "bounty" to be exacted from agricultural production. An educational plan such as we have been talking about presupposes industrial policies that take agriculture as their necessary base, not their dependent servant. With a strong base in agricultural production, peasants and urban industrial workers are producing for the social and collective well-being of the society as a whole.[14] If this is not the case and if agriculture is weak, then a great gap is created between the standards of living of the two groups. All this, of course, is related to the basic concepts governing production.

If profit continues to have a prominent role in this concept, similar to its role in capitalist economy, production will be oriented in the direction of the values of exchange and not toward the values of use. Thus it will not be surprising that the stimulus to production will always be of a material nature, contrary to the central thrust of an educational program such as the one we have been discussing here. A program linked to production that seeks to build such social incentives as cooperative work and concern for the common good places its faith in human beings. It has a critical, not ingenuous, belief in the ability of people to be remade in the process of reconstructing their society.

One of the advantages of a project such as the one I have been proposing is that it invites critical reflection on a contextual reality as one lives with it. It calls for a type of school in harmony with the plan for a new society in Guinea-Bissau and the Cape Verde Islands: a school that does not divide theory from practice, reflection from action, intellectual work from manual labor.

It seems to me that the old school which dichotomizes everything should be abolished as soon as possible wherever it exists. Such a school should never be permitted to be started in areas that do not yet know its alienating presence.

About a year ago I had the opportunity to observe a really rich experiment in a rural zone in the Caribbean. Some features of that experiment—especially the way in which the peasants were organizing their own education—can offer valuable suggestions to the project we are discussing here.

The peasants, organized in a production cooperative,* di-

---

*This cooperative was born in the midst of a conflict between the peasants and a foreign corporation that exploited the land and the peasant work force. The incident that provoked the conflict was the dismissal of a national agronomist, recently hired, with whom the peasants were completely united due to the open and democratic manner that characterized his work with them. The conflict gave rise to a prolonged strike—the first in the area—that ended in the nationalization of all the land exploited by foreign corporations. Only a part of that land was then "ceded" to the peasants in an arrangement whereby they paid by cultivating the land.

vided the area to be cultivated into work units with a minimum of 15 workers assigned to each. In each of these areas they constructed a small shelter to serve as a restaurant and study center. Two or three women (since they had not yet overcome the prejudice against men cooking) prepared the lunch. Each of the workers brought some contribution of food when they came to work early in the morning—a chicken, a fish, a piece of meat, vegetables or fruit. At the lunch hour no one had the right to reclaim his own original contribution. All ate what had been prepared from the common meal. Solidarity in work was translated into a common meal.

Each group elected a leader, who worked in the same way as the others in the fields but had the responsibility to organize the work, to coordinate it and, sometimes, to represent the others before the administration, which was also made up of peasants.

They gave themselves two hours for lunch, during which time they invariably discussed a wide range of problems—techniques of agriculture, health problems, finances, business concerns, and the political dimension of all of these problems. They evaluated their own practice. I attended one of these meetings and can testify once again to the obvious: in thinking about practice, we learn to think correctly.

Once a week the group leaders meet with the agricultural engineer (who goes to the fields daily) and together they make an evaluation of the week's work. In the next meeting with their groups, the leaders make an analysis of their meeting with the agronomist who, while he is a functionary of the cooperative, is the peasant's own technician.

Besides these meetings of the groups and of the leaders with the agronomist, there are other administrative meetings of the directors of the cooperative as well as some special meetings. The president, himself a peasant, discusses with his companions general lines of action, urgent problems that they face, and whatever other matters may come up for attention.

After a time of working in this way, the peasants decided to broaden the experience. They began to motivate the population of a small urban center nearby which was closely related to their rural area. They now offer four seminars annually that begin with an analysis of their own experience and include a broader range of problems within the local reality. The peasants decide on the agenda for these meetings and also choose some of their number to be the presenters of brief communications that are followed by general discussion.

During my visit I stayed in the home of the president of the cooperative. I took part in one of those seminars for the urban population. I was not at all surprised by the lucid manner in which the peasants spoke on the various themes of the seminar: their criticism of individualism, opportunism and personalism; their emphasis on the necessity of cooperative work; their repudiation of vertical solutions; their defense of their right to have a voice in what happens; the manner in which their political practice had radicalized them; their insight that the causes of their most fundamental problems could not always be found in the few acres that they cultivated. They had come little by little to a vision of the whole, overcoming a localized version of their situation.

As I write this letter, I have no idea whether this experiment has been aborted, or, if it continues, whether it has been distorted. Neither of these hypotheses would surprise me.

It is interesting to observe, however, the way in which this experiment, described so briefly, takes us back to points we have discussed before. One of these is the role of conflict in the clarification of political consciousness. The same peasants whom I saw so actively organizing in behalf of their interests had been apathetic only a few years before.

We can see how rich the liberation struggle in Guinea-Bissau has been as we look at its consequences in the political clarity of the people.

The relation between education and the transformation of infrastructures is another case in point. Before the conflict that resulted in the creation of the cooperative and thus altered the social relations of those engaged in production, the same peasant population had neither the objective nor subjective conditions for an educational undertaking. But, given the new conditions, it was possible to initiate an activity that broke down the old division between practice and theory, action and reflection, manual and intellectual work.

Finally, the experiment shows the possibility for a whole production area to become one great Culture Circle in which all are
educated and all educate, taking their own practice as the starting point for analysis and critical comprehension of daily life.

Let us summarize the principal points we have made in this
letter about a possible project. These are not meant to be rigid
prescriptions, but merely a recapping of the principal points:

1. Choose an area that is already a natural unity in terms of
what is cultivated; let it become one large Culture Circle.

2. The local population, from the beginning of its mobilization, should feel that the project belongs to them and should
have a role in its administration. Careful interpretation of the
objectives and of certain of the methodologies to be used are
important. Young people who have recently graduated from the
lycée should be incorporated into the project whenever possible. They should become part of the local population, understanding their action as part of their "death"—their rejection of
intellectual formation that takes place far from productive work
and from the people who engage in it. Their acceptance as true
comrades of that population is essential. Young members of the
armed forces who have been demobilized may also become
engaged in this work. For them it may be easier, since they may
come from rural areas and they also may have experience in
literacy and post-literacy education. Since many of these young
persons with lycée education were not able to participate in the
liberation struggle, this participation would be their contribution to the struggle for national reconstruction. Two years of
productive work and engagement in political-pedagogical
efforts side by side with their peasant comrades would give them
what the lycée could never offer, no matter how well intentioned
their professors. Sometimes these young people might go to
Bissau to participate in seminars with students and teachers at
the lycée on such topics as the experiment in which they are
participating. On such occasions, they should be accompanied
by some of the peasants with whom they work. They would thus
be motivating other young persons by their example. This practice would have implications for the reformation of the educational system of the country.

3. The programmatic content of education emerges from a

permanent process of critical reflection. Social practice, especially that related to production, is one of the determining factors. Analysis of practice in production opens the possibility for
serious study that can move gradually to a deeper level, the level
of the basic reason for things. This rich and pluralistic theme
begins with simple matters of agricultural techniques—planting, the harvest, treatment of the land, combating insects and
other plagues, erosion. It goes on to an understanding of the
act of production itself. The political economy of the country—
what, why, and how to produce—health problems and preventive medicine can all be considered. Discussions of preventive
medicine could lead to the provision of special training by the
Commission on Health for local "folk doctors," resulting in new
and better medical services for the local population. We need
not list here all the possible themes that emerge from reflection
on production practices. It is enough to note that their number
is limitless. They can become a series of interrelated units in the
programmatic content of education. The most important consideration is that they never be treated as finished formulas,
statistics or bureaucratic answers. The answer is part of an open
search by the participants and belongs to them.

4. To put such a project into practice would require the collaboration of all of the Commissions—Education, Agriculture,
Health, Communication, Finances, Commerce. The Party, in its
local, regional and national organization, should not only be
aware of the project but constantly informed of its progress. In
some situations the Party would initiate the project locally in
cooperation with the appropriate Commissions. When the possibility of such a project is first discussed, all who are to be
related to it should be present; their participation should continue through the training of educators and at every stage of the
project's progress.

5. It is obvious that the relation to the local committee of the
area is essential. Actual practice will reveal the best ways to
establish and maintain this relation, and that with the Commissions, in the least bureaucratic, most efficient manner.

6. The degree to which it is possible to carry out such an
experiment in any given area with the full participation of the

population will determine how it can be transformed into an example for others and a center for the training of leaders.

7. Actual practice will teach all those who are engaged in it to see a wide variety of aspects and problems never mentioned in this letter and, certainly, to rectify errors in the suggestions given here. Wherever possible, the debates and discussions that take place in the groups should be recorded for learning and for other reasons described in earlier letters.

*Fraternally,*
*Paulo Freire*

# Letter 16

Geneva
May 7, 1976

Engineer Mario Cabral
Commissioner of State for Education and Culture
Bissau, Republic of Guinea-Bissau

*Comrade Mario Cabral,*
    Once more I want to say how sorry Elza and I were not to be able to be with you on the occasion of the last visit of the IDAC team.

There follows a copy of a letter that I have written to Paulo and, through him, to the whole team. As you will see when you read it, my intention has been to put certain problems on the table, to examine them in the light of the practice in which we are involved together, and not to offer solutions.

If you should find anything in the letter that does not correspond to reality in the country and with which, for this reason, you cannot agree, please call my attention to it so that I can correct it and work better because of that.

As I said in the letter I sent through Miguel, we are awaiting your instructions about sending funds.

Hoping to meet you in Dar es Salaam next month, I send the embrace of your friend and comrade,

*Paulo*

# Letter 17

Geneva
Spring of 1976

*Dear Paulo,*

A few days ago I received your letter in which you spoke of having meetings related to different specialties within the field of adult literacy.

I do not want to appear too insistent, but I must mention again my sense of the importance of working together across lines of specialization. Nor do I want to overemphasize what is obvious to all of us—the enrichment that comes from the exchange of experiences. I am convinced that the difficulties you are confronting have an easy solution. There is one common denominator that all of you have in common—your militant stance. The truth is that the more militant we become through clarifying our political practice and our loyalties, knowing whose side we are on and to whom we are committed, the more able we are to overcome individualistic temptations that make teamwork difficult. Militants are much more than specialists. Militancy forces us to be more disciplined and to try harder to understand the reality that we, together with other militants, are trying to transform and re-create. We stand together, alert against threats of all kinds.

In this sense, a meeting of militants to evaluate their own

practice—not *for* but *with* the people—cannot possibly become a meeting of specialists who feel a need to defend themselves against each other. A meeting of militants is characterized by dialogue, not by polemic. This should not suggest that there are not differences in points of view, but these are to be overcome in serious discussions.

In my conversations with educators, I have always stressed the need for political clarity—especially with regard to whose interests they are serving—rather than techniques and methods.

Militancy teaches us that pedagogical problems are, first of all, political and ideological—no matter how much this statement may upset those educators fond of talking in the most abstract terms about education and those who dream of inventing a model human being completely free of all the concrete conditions in which human beings are presently immersed.

The new man and the new woman will not be constructed in the heads of educators but in a new social practice, which will take the place of the old that has proven itself incapable of creating new persons.

Correct militancy also demands the dialectical unity between practice and theory, action and reflection. This unity stimulates creativity, the best protection against the dangers of bureaucratization.

My own deep involvement with the themes that have been the object of my concern have never bureaucratized my curiosity about them. I approach the themes but at the same time take a distance from them, treating them as problem statements and thus as challenges whose meaning is to be revealed.

In the act of revealing them, or seeing them again, I must reexamine also the perception I had of them when I reflected on them in the past. And further, I see again and examine again the practice that was mine with regard to these themes, my current practice, and the practice of others. All this becomes the object of my current analyses. In such a practice, the themes are always seen as problems.

The point of reference for my reflection is practice: my curiosity can never become bureaucratized so long as my practice does not become so. Thus, the permanent exercise of reflection, which I take as a discipline, is always oriented toward the concrete problems in which I am involved. When I try to withdraw from the concrete problems and make them into themes on which to reflect, to understand their reason for being, I can never accept the temptation to transform them into vague abstractions. The moment that I accept that temptation, I become disconnected with my own practice, denying its key role in my own reflection. Reflection on abstractions becomes a purely intellectual exercise. I may make some pronouncement—profound or empty, but always meaningless when it is divorced from the reality of practice.

The dialectic unity between action and reflection, practice and theory, imposes itself on my being, whether the context in which I find myself is concrete or theoretical. In "taking a distance," I do so simply to examine better what is actually going on wherever I am.

It is for this reason that I keep insisting that the practice of thinking about practice is the best way to think correctly.

I do not wish to be in the position of lecturing you or giving advice, but I do feel impelled to say that this critical reflection on your practice, required by true militancy, should probably be the central concern of the Commission that brings you all together in the first meetings that you described in your letter.

I would like to take advantage of this opportunity, also, to mention a point that came up frequently in the meetings we had in February (1976) when we were last with you. In those meetings the evidence was that the work of adult literacy education in the heavily populated areas of Bissau was yielding far fewer results than that realized within FARP, although the effort expended was almost the same.

Even though we can recognize the principal reasons for this divergence of results, I think it may be important to go back and reflect again on what has been done to date. This may help us to come up with some new ways to make the work among civilians more effective. I recognize that you have already begun this process. I am simply adding my own thoughts.

It is evident that one of the major reasons for the rapid advance of literacy efforts within FARP is the high level of political awareness among the military growing out of the long struggle for liberation.

It should not surprise us that these militants understand the necessity of learning to read and write as one way in which they can serve the cause of national reconstruction, which for them is a natural continuation of the earlier struggle. They are not motivated by personal interests but by the cause that they serve. What would be strange, indeed, would be their looking on literacy as the means to better employment and positions of privilege. For them the term "national reconstruction" has a concrete meaning. That meaning was made clear for them in the midst of the struggle. In it they must have understood the warning of Amilcar Cabral: "The people do not fight for ideas or anything that is simply in men's heads. They accept the sacrifices required by the struggle in order to be able to live better and in peace. They want to guarantee the future and progress for their children. Without that, national liberation, the fight against colonialism, independence, and even peace and progress themselves are empty terms. They have no significance if they cannot be translated into real improvements in the conditions of their lives."[15]

One time when Elza and I were visiting one of the Culture Circles in FARP the discussion was about certain events in the liberation struggle and their relation to national reconstruction. One of the participants remarked, "If during reconstruction the struggle to increase production requires us to eat only once a day, then we will eat only once a day. The interests of the whole people are more important than our own interests individually."

Whatever illiteracy exists within FARP is linguistic and not political. From a political point of view these military personnel are highly literate, unlike so many so-called literate persons who are illiterates politically.

One of the characteristics of PAIGC has been its understanding of national liberation as "a cultural fact and a factor of culture." There was never a dichotomy between politics and the military.

Not just once or twice but many times Amilcar Cabral emphasized in his writings that "our armed resistance is a political
act," and "our armed resistance is also an expression of our
cultural resistance."[16]

It was this dynamic understanding of the struggle, formed
within the struggle itself, that led Amilcar Cabral and his comrades of the Party to place such importance on the rigorous
training of the military. That training was never reduced simply
to the use of arms. The soldier learned not only what a gun was
and how to use it but also what it was being used for, why it was
used, against whom, against what, and in whose behalf it was
being used.

"We are militants and not merely military men," said Cabral.
He insisted on "effective political work at the heart of the armed
forces." "Lacking that," he said, "a certain military mindset can
be created. Such a tendency must be rooted out should it ever
appear."

The militants of FARP, whatever their rank, learned to reflect
on the struggle. To serve in FARP meant, above all, to be a
militant constantly challenged to think, to learn, to criticize and
to be criticized. It meant to be able to learn from one's achievements and from one's errors. This was the climate of the struggle.

In one of his writings Cabral said, "We must develop the
principle of criticism in all of the meetings of the Party, in all
of our committees, and in the armed forces—among guerrilla
troops as well as among the military. After every action against
the enemy, we should look at the results and at the part played
by every combatant."[17] On another occasion he said, "We must
increase our consciousness of our errors and failures in order
to correct what we do and make our service to the Party constantly better. Our errors should not discourage us just as our
victories should not make us forget the errors." Later, he remarked, "In the light of the promises of the struggle, we need
to study every problem in depth and find the best solution. We
must think in order to act and act in order to think better."[18]

This understanding of militancy and of commitment that includes critical curiosity and the need to understand more and

more clearly the reality that is being transformed continues to characterize FARP. It could not be otherwise at this critical moment in national life. It is this understanding of militancy, with all that it implies, that enables us to understand the highly positive results in literacy and post-literacy education within FARP.

The situation that we confront among civilians in Bissau is quite different. That population was exposed to the power and presence of the colonizers—both to their seduction and their violence. That population was untouched, or almost untouched, by the struggle and was never politically awakened.*
While it is natural for the militants of FARP to see literacy and post-literacy as parts of their political response to the collective interests of the people, the majority of civilians—as the data seem to tell us—see literacy as the solution to their individual problems.

Even though we are convinced that this attitude will be overcome to the degree that the Party, faithful to its own past and to the commitment it has made to the government and to the people, continues to give witness to this faithfulness through improved material conditions, we cannot neglect the concrete data. If, in speaking of the liberation struggle, Cabral reminded us that the people will not fight for vague ideas but only for substantial improvements, in their lives, then we must remember the same words during national reconstruction and relate them to the process of adult literacy education.

We therefore have a series of problems facing us as we plan for literacy education in the civilian area: What should be our approach? How do we make a problematic of the natural individualistic perception of literacy? How can we, beginning with our very first contacts with the people, begin to link literacy to some concrete tasks to be accomplished through mutual help, rather than perpetuate the present perception of it as an intel-

---

*This observation does not in any sense deny the efforts of PAIGC in Bissau beginning in 1956, the year of its founding. Nor does it deny the terrible repression of the colonial powers against the first signs of popular rebellion, including the massacre of Pidjiguiti in 1959. PAIGC made great efforts to work with the population in Bissau.

lectual activity that contributes to individual progress?

In beginning to rethink the activities in this area, I believe that the Commission should exercise extreme care in selecting a few sites for experimental work and make there some new approaches to literacy education. One reason for the careful selection process is that we know that whatever results can be obtained there will play an important role in the whole campaign and may condition its expansion to other areas. We will need to learn from the experiments and to analyze and discuss the reasons behind whatever accomplishments or errors occur. It will also mean applying to our literacy efforts—both to their organization and functioning—the same militant, creative discipline that Cabral described as fundamental to victory in the liberation struggle.

The selection process will, naturally, be based on certain criteria. I would suggest at least two: that the population of the area be involved in some systematic, productive activity—or about to begin such an effort—and that the present level of political participation of the population be considered. What has been their response to political mobilization by the neighborhood Party committee? The Party must, of course, have an important role not only in the choice of areas but in the implementation of the program.

After the areas are chosen—two or three, the number doesn't matter—the first step would be a visit to the neighborhood by members of the Commission, accompanied by representatives of the local political committee.

At this point it would perhaps be appropriate to say why you are visiting the area and to explain something about the literacy work to be undertaken. You could say whether you live in Bissau and if you have been to that neighborhood before. The fact of having visited a neighborhood or even walked its streets daily does not necessarily mean that one has a really critical vision of the neighborhood. We begin to get that kind of vision only when we do more than simply visit or walk through the streets looking and listening. When we take the neighborhood or the street as our own concern, trying to *see* them and to *hear* what the people are saying, then we communicate with them. We become more than cool, distant specialists who analyze the inhabitants of the area. We become militants in search of the reality of the area *with* the people who live there.

In these visits the smallest details should be noticed: the condition of the streets; the health of the people; whether or not there are places where people gather and talk with each other; the way the children play in the streets. These and an infinite number of facts will be revealed to us when we no longer simply walk through the streets but, rather, become curious about them.

It would be possible to take photographs of some of these aspects of the neighborhood—true codifications of the area—which might be discussed later by the participants in the Culture Circles.

In these visits we make our first critical approach to the *barrios* and begin our understanding of them. It is an understanding that will become real in proportion to our intimacy with the people who live there, not only in the Culture Circles but, above all, in some concrete action program planned with the people themselves.

In some cases we may want to begin with the post-literacy phase, that is, with discussions about concrete aspects of life in the *barrio* and the ways in which people might work together to resolve small local problems. If, for example, one of the needs were to fill in holes in the streets where water collects, becomes stagnant and provides a breeding place for mosquitoes, then various other factors affecting public health could also be considered. Beyond this, the value of helping each other and working together to resolve problems could be examined. Such discussions move from the particular needs for reconstruction within the *barrio* to the reconstruction of the *barrio* itself.

At a certain point in the people's engagement with concrete tasks, the necessity for literacy begins to be perceived. What we have called "post-literacy" in this case preceded literacy. In any situation it is very important to relate literacy and post-literacy to some practical activity that both serves common interests and is undertaken cooperatively. There is no guaranteed prescription nor ready-made project that can be suggested. Only in living with the people in their *barrio* will we discover with them what needs doing. In working together on the task and thinking about what we do, we will learn more and better.

The programmatic content of literacy education—the generative words and the themes related to them—emerge from a critical understanding of the *barrio* and of the different practices that can be developed within it.

As I have said so many times, even when I suggest certain lines of action, I do not mean to do more than to propose some questions. My intention is not to offer solutions.

It is in this spirit that I write you now when you are looking for new ways to make your literacy work with adults in Bissau more dynamic.

*With the fraternal embrace of*
*Paulo Freire*

# POSTSCRIPT

Working visits to Saõ Tomé e Principe and to Angola in December 1976 and February 1977, and the first trip this year to Guinea-Bissau (March 1977), coincided with my final revision of the introduction and preparation of the letters that make up this book. The meetings that I had at that time with the Coordinating Commission on Adult Literacy, with the teachers studying at Có and the permanent staff and directors there, as well as with others responsible for the various activities of the Commission on Education, convinced me of the necessity for this postscript. In writing it, I shall try to restrain myself from going into minute details regarding the conversations that Elza, Julio de Santa Ana of the Commission on the Churches' Participation in Development and I had with the people at Có. What I hope to do is simply to bring up to date some of the considerations, analyses, and information contained in the Introduction.

## The Relation between Education and Production

I want to highlight first the relation between education and production to which I made reference so insistently in the introduction. This relation is a primary concern for PAIGC and for the government through the Commission on Education. In a recent interview with the *Lisbon Daily*, Mario Cabral said, "Of all of our efforts and our tasks in the Commission on Education, the relation between production and education is the one that has most affected me and the one I most like to talk about."[1]

This preoccupation with not permitting education to be separated from production has been characteristic of the work of PAIGC in the older liberated zones during the long struggle. It cannot help becoming a central factor, a type of "generative theme," on which the new educational system for the country is founded. It was for this reason that, in the beginning of the academic year in 1975, only a few months after the entry of PAIGC into Bissau, the Commission on Education took the first steps to bring about this unity while, at the same time, working to maintain and stimulate it in the liberated zones.

Mario Cabral and his closest colleagues—among them Carlos Dias, who is responsible for promoting the relation between work and study—knew that it would be impossible to replace the inherited educational system if the teaching were all verbal and the students kept at a distance from the productive act. At the same time, however, they understood the ideological reasons for the resistance of some students. In a matter so fundamental and delicate for the future of the country, we can see once again the wisdom that PAIGC had been accumulating during the years of struggle. The solution they sought can be discerned in the balance between impatience and patience and in forms of action impatiently patient. There was no question, at that stage, of imposing on students in the lycée in Bissau the requirement that they participate in productive labor. The question was rather one of convincing them of the formative value of work. What was being required at that time was the attempt to win the students for the task of reinventing their own society, within which the unity of work and study would be indispensable.

This was, in fact, the principal objective of the Commission on Education when it proposed to the students in Bissau in the beginning of the school year in 1975 the first projects based on unity between their activities of study and production. One conviction was firm for the Commission when it initiated dialogue with the youth. That conviction was, of course, that without that unity of study and work built into the new social practice that was being formed, it would not be possible to create a new society in which the differences between manual and so-called intellectual work could be overcome. Any society that dreams of becoming a society of workers must have as its basis full employment and the production of socially useful goods, since these are fundamental in the formation of the new man and the new woman.

Carlos Dias observed in one of our conversations that "it would be impossible to conceive of work apart from education as though it were something to which we aspired or which we were preparing ourselves to do in the future instead of understanding it to be the very center of the formative process. Therefore to work while studying and to study while working has become our theme." This concept has nothing to do with the work-study programs in capitalist societies, where, in the centers for industrial apprenticeship, future workers are prepared to sell their labor to the industrial class.

"In the transition from the society in which we now live to one without exploiters or exploited," says Carlos Dias, "there are two objectives of the relation between study and work—work that is useful, rich and creative: one is to throw light on the contradiction between manual work and intellectual work, since we are still far from overcoming the separation between the two; the other is to make possible the gradual self-financing of education, without which it will not be possible to make it truly democratic under present conditions in our society."

If, as I suggested, this was the firm conviction of the Commissioner for Education when he established the first dialogues with youth of middle-school age in Bissau, his confidence in the young people themselves was equally strong. He believed in youth and in the fact that young people could be challenged (not threatened) to assume their proper role in the task of national reconstruction. He did not have some vague, diffuse confidence that might result from an opportunist position. Nor did he have an ingenuous certainty that, left to themselves, the youth would discover with clarity their role in that task. Rather, his was a critical confidence—very similar to that of those practical political pedagogues Amilcar Cabral, Samora Machel, Fidel, Nakarenko, Freinet, Nyerere—to name just a few among so many.

When he began his dialogue with the students of the lycée, the Commissioner knew that a few would accept his invitation and enter into the first experiments in productive work. The testimony of this small group, along with continuing political work, would communicate to the rest.

The initiatives begun in 1975 did indeed spread during the year, and by March 1976 the number of participating students had reached a surprising level. The small minority who had started in 1975 had given themselves to productive labor and had become, in 1976, the majority of students at the Bissau lycée. Today 800 students from this school are organized in committees, elect their own leaders, and are fully engaged in productive work. During my last visit, I used to see them, early in the morning, spreading throughout the city in groups, disciplined and happy. Some walked in the direction of the fields around the Simão Mendes Hospital, 25 minutes from the school; others went on their way to fields in a rural area outside the city, even further away than the hospital. The very presence of these students moving through the streets of the city with their farming implements on their shoulders is a new "language" that announces the construction of a new society. It provides a testimony to the fact that something new is happening in the city. Young persons have stopped "consuming" their studies, memorizing the geography and history of the metropolitan culture in order to find in their work the basis for their learning.

In a month they dedicated 1,377 hours of labor to the Simão Mendes Hospital, 2,187 hours to the farming near Antuta, a few kilometers from Bissau, and 1,908 hours to an area where the work is sponsored by the Commission on Commerce and Crafts.

Some of the students who work in the fields around the hospital plant flowers for the sick. They learn to think about the meaning of those roses and the message they carry to those who are seriously ill. They put the same love into that work and into the preparation of the land for planting fruit trees. They learn a love of life that influences their effort toward the revolutionary reconstruction of their society.

In the interior of the country, due to the people's longer participation in the struggle, the facts are even more eloquent. In Tombali, for example, adolescents planted 917 banana trees, harvested 1,020 kilos of rice, and prepared 837 square meters of land for cultivation. In Bedanda, in the same region, much more land has been prepared for planting.

Bafatá continues to be the model region and the best organized. By 1974 most of the schools in Bafatá already had their own farm area. Now every school has one. Students and teachers together planted and harvested 24,516 kilos of potatoes; 4,823 kilos of rice; 11,177 kilos of wheat; 800 kilos of peanuts and 250 of beans.

Productive work, because it is visibly collective, gives teachers and students a clear vision of goals for their own development. It enables communities to view the school as something that emerges from their own life, not something that is "outside" or "above" them. The school is clearly perceived to be serving the whole national community. "At the moment," says Carlos Dias, "our greatest preoccupation is to develop the school's fields and the fields of the student's families in one united productive enterprise. In Bula we are beginning experiments in which the peasant farmers, the students, and the military of FARP give themselves to productive work as collectives."

It is important to emphasize that all of this is only in its beginning stages. Even though they cannot hide their satisfaction with the results that they are obtaining, Mario Cabral and his colleagues are very aware of all that remains to be done in this as in every other sector affecting the national education system. When they spoke to us of what is already happening in the country and when they accompanied us to see in concrete ways the progress of which they spoke, they still did not let themselves fall into an ingenuous euphoria, nor did they lose their humility. In sharing with us the analyses of what is being done toward national reconstruction, they spoke with the same revolutionary modesty that was present in their references to that earlier phase, the liberation struggle.

Within the overall theme of the relation between study and work, there is an experiment in adult literacy education that, according to all indications, promises to become an example for other regions of the country. It cannot, of course, be transplanted and copied, but it can become a site where others can learn. Not only the Commission members can learn from it, but our team also.

The experiment is rich due to the variety of factors interwoven in it that can be considered, analyzed and followed in their minute details. One of them, for example, resembles the experience of Tachai to which I referred in Letter 15. The dynamic relationship that has been established between education and the socio-economic transformations taking place mean that each influences and motivates changes in the other.

A further example is that in some instances what we customarily refer to as "post-literacy" is actually preceding basic literacy work. This is an instance of what I have always believed, namely, that the literacy education of adults is really a process of cultural action.* The "reading" or "rereading" of reality as it is being transformed is the primary consideration, taking precedence over the mere learning of the written language. Even in teaching children, the process is social and involves "reading" the world.

It is not always necessary that the "reading" of reality be a parallel process with learning to read linguistic symbols, that is, with literacy as it is generally understood. In certain circumstances, it is possible that a community engage for a period of time in a series of practical reflections on their own reality, discussing generative themes related to their concrete interests. They may discuss, for example, their experience with collective production of what they need and the relationship between this activity and national reconstruction. They would thus be involved in what we have generally thought of as post-literacy before they have begun to turn their attention to their need to learn linguistic symbols. In this case, it would be through reflection on their own situation that they would be impelled to begin the process of learning to deal with written words. For them it

---

*The very designation "Culture Circles" rather than "adult literacy classes" was intended to emphasize this point.

might have been impossible to reverse the process.

There are, of course, other situations where learning to read and write is what motivates the learners to mobilize and organize themselves for some action that, until this point, has seemed unnecessary, impossible or, even, unknown to them.

Mobilization and organization for action are a response to what had previously been a need that was only "felt" but which becomes, in the present, a challenge, something that stands out on its own. It is as though they had made a real discovery. And from this moment forward, the project that is undertaken, which was born in the midst of literacy education, itself changes the educational practice that gave it birth.

All of this characterizes the experiment that, beginning in October 1975, has been developing in the Sedengal region in the extreme north of the country. Its history began when the Coordinating Commission on Adult Literacy found that a large group of students at the lycée in Bissau who came from the interior of the country had great interest in participating in literacy programs. The Commission, taking advantage of this interest and of the opportunity provided by a long vacation period, made it possible for them to go out to work in what were called brigades. Two hundred students engaged in this work.

When they went home on vacation to their own regions they put in practice the central objectives of the brigades. They never worked individually, but in teams, coordinated by one of their own number. Working in areas that had been designated as priority zones, the students began to mobilize local communities. They interpreted the meaning of literacy and in this way interested some of the local young people, who were then trained by the brigades. Work was begun in the certainty that it would be carried on, because the real leadership was passing to local young persons who could carry on when the brigades left.

Not all of the brigades realized their objectives. For some, their own training in Bissau lacked any significant practice, and this lack meant that the theory they were espousing was somewhat empty. In other cases, the mobilization of the communities was not so well planned as it might have been, nor were the

PEDAGOGY IN PROCESS

necessary measures for maintaining enthusiasm and motivation really carried out. But, on the whole, the effort was valid because it gave rise to such successful experiments as that in Sedengal, and it also provided a great deal of data from which the Coordinating Commission could learn as it analyzed both positive and negative outcomes. The members of the brigades also learned a lot from their participation. Some of them were motivated to continue working in the field of adult literacy during the school term in Bissau and in the countryside during their vacations.

The mobilization of the local population in the communities —intended as the basis for organizing literacy programs—included attempts to get at their basic needs. While this assessment of needs was not thorough or rigorous, it was important because the people took part in the data gathering. They were not merely objects being studied by someone else.

In the analysis of the experience of the brigades, the important role taken by the local Party committees was again made clear. Not that their cooperation can assure the success of any venture, but without their cooperation very little can happen. In the case of Sedengal, the local committee was deeply involved from the beginning in the mobilization of the population and in the census of needs.

In actual fact, of course, the population of Sedengal was not mobilized by the brigade nor by the local committee of PAIGC. They mobilized themselves. The organization of the Culture Circles in which the participants began to read their own reality and to learn to read and write letters was carried out by the learners and by the community at large. The effective assumption of responsibility by the community actually gave such strength to the project that its success was assured. The full participation of the community resulted in a large number of young people from the area being trained by the brigade as leaders in the Culture Circles. These young people had only three or four years of schooling themselves. They were born and had grown up in Sedengal. They became involved with their older comrades in the process of "rereading" and "rewriting" the world of Sedengal, not merely in the reading and writing of words. These same young people sometimes walked from one community to another ten kilometers distant to sell baskets and mats that they had produced themselves. With their earnings they bought kerosene to light the lamps used by the Culture Circles for their night sessions. This assumption of responsibility by the community meant that the majority of the population was always present in the periodic meetings of the Coordinating Commission with the young leaders of the Culture Circles. Although only the leaders were essential to these evaluation meetings, the whole community participated because of their interest in what was going on.

All indications are that that community will become one large Culture Circle. This hypothesis is becoming a reality because, beginning with actual experience in the Culture Circles as they "read" reality and learn from it and as they make their first precarious steps in the learning of reading and writing, they have moved toward the discovery of the need to dedicate themselves to a major project—that of cultivating some land that belongs to the State, four or five kilometers away from their settlement, working it as a collective.*

From that point on they organized themselves, dividing into small teams responsible for different aspects of the work. They interpreted their project to everyone in the community and obtained complete participation. They joined forces to acquire work tools; they discussed what to produce and started preparing the earth for planting. In this way, they began to "rewrite" their own reality. They moved from individual to collective work. "Anyone not committed to working together would be out of place in Sedengal today," observed one of them in a meeting with the members of the Coordinating Commission.

One of the members of this Commission said to me in March 1977 that "enthusiasm is the characteristic mark of the population of Sedengal. Enthusiasm—a certain joy in living—like that which comes over us when we have discovered something entirely new and we ask ourselves how it was ever possible to live

---

*The Commission on Agriculture is extending technical assistance to this project.

without this for so long. It is as though it were something that had been latent in us, awaiting the proper moment to appear. The discovery constitutes a moment whose time has come. It is in this way that I see the people of Sedengal, their enthusiasm, the uncontained joy they feel in the face of 'their' new thing—collective work. For them the discovery of the collective approach to work has not negated individual effort. It has enriched it. On the other hand," she continued, "collective efforts have visibly raised the political consciousness of the population. In a recent meeting in Sedengal when we mentioned the Third Congress of the Party, the people talked about their contribution and agreed that the best contribution they might make would be to extend and perfect collective work in their own locale."

This same comrade from the Coordinating Commission went on to say, "Sedengal is a place of surprises. It is impossible to go there without being challenged by something new. We have to run here and there with the local people, learning with them, because they are the ones who are inventing something new. One of them actually remarked recently, 'We never knew before what we knew. Now we not only know what we knew, but we also know that we are able to know a lot more.' "

The experiment in adult literacy education as cultural action resulted in the discovery by the people of Sedengal of the power of collectivity. The whole population became engaged in cooperative work. The dynamic interaction between the Culture Circles and productive labor was established and flourished in the collective "gardens."

It would be too much to hope, however, that the experience of collective production could, by itself, overcome the very fundamental problem of language. The people of Sedengal understand and speak Creole. They have no experience with Portuguese at all. This constitutes a very real barrier not only for Sedengal but for other areas of the country. Mario Cabral made this very clear in the last meeting of the Coordinating Commission.

A full understanding of the difficulties confronted by the Commission on Education of Guinea-Bissau in the task of adult literacy education must include this particular problem and another of equal magnitude that is sometimes forgotten: the unusually large difference that exists between the number of the population that can actually read and write and those who can't. One of the legacies of colonialism after five centuries of "assistance" in Guinea is the fact that 90 to 95 percent of the population was left unlettered.

In any case, in the bilingual and even trilingual zones where Creole is one of the languages, the learning of Portuguese is taking place without major difficulties. The situation in FARP, where there is practically no remaining illiteracy, is a case in point.

One impression that remains with me is that in the case of Sedengal the dynamic relation between the Culture Circles and collective production will continue but that the interest in learning Portuguese will, at a certain point, diminish greatly in the face of the difficulties they will meet. I say this not dogmatically but as the result of my reflection on what I see happening. If this does happen, it will not signify a major tragedy. It will not be sufficient reason for the Coordinating Commission to bid a sad farewell to the people of Sedengal and go away frustrated. Their task of cultural action will continue. The domination of language as a total system of expression will remain. The experience of Sedengal will simply reaffirm what we know already: that it is possible to "read" and to "rewrite" reality without learning to read and write linguistic symbols.

## Activities in the People's Revolutionary Army (FARP)

Within FARP a number of activities now represent the actual carrying out of some of the ideas referred to in the introduction. Many of my remarks are based on the analysis of these activities as reported to us in a meeting with the Political Commissioner of the Army, Julio de Carvalho, and his immediate assistants. Their present preoccupation is focused on several precise areas. One of these is the post-literacy phase of their work.

Only recently has it been possible to intensify the post-literacy program, first in Bissau, and to assure its extension to other areas of the country. The support materials necessary for this work now exist. I refer to the basic manuals—one containing orientation information and suggestions for the leaders of Culture Circles, and the other furnishing the texts with themes to be analyzed and discussed in the process of making a "critical reading" of national reality. In post-literacy this effort was begun and now must be extended to include African reality. Mathematical studies, like calculus, are also developed in this material.

The learners themselves played an important part in the organization of this manual. Most of the texts were drawn from recordings of debates that took place in the Culture Circles during the process of decoding the situations to which the generative words referred. The team responsible for preparing the manual edited, organized and systematized the material in a language that was not too far removed from that of the learners. The manual represented an attempt to return to the learners, in an organized form, texts representing their own earlier analyses. They were actually codifications with some new elements added. When the learners were "invited" in the post-literacy phase to make a critical analysis of the texts, they were actually analyzing a synthesis of their earlier analyses. The leaders in the Bissau zone also made their contribution. The team responsible for the manual gathered them in groups and went over the material text by text. In this way the leaders, through their participation in the development not only of the texts themselves but of their content, were involved in a training process that prepared them for the next phase of their work. The principal task of the leader would be to use the text as a tool that would challenge the learner and leader alike to a new analysis. One of the real risks of this model of teaching and learning is that the text itself may become a kind of "reading lesson," a substitute for the struggle to penetrate the structures of reality that it represents. For this reason, much emphasis has been placed on the training of leaders and on their constant retraining through evaluation seminars dealing with their actual practices.

In the area of post-literacy in FARP there is an experiment

being carried on with some clear implications. It is one in which there is close cooperation between FARP and the Commission on Education. Two hundred military personnel are involved; they had their first initiation into reading and writing during the liberation struggle in the midst of the wilderness where they were located. Having participated from the beginning in the literacy program of the armed forces, these 200 were able, after the total independence of the country, to review their learning during the struggle and to move quickly into what FARP usually calls the transition period leading to post-literacy work.

"The project," said Julio de Carvalho, "gave us an opportunity to conduct an evaluation, in a very untraditional manner, that enabled us to enter the universe of knowledge of these comrades and to understand how they see reality, including African reality, and to discover their levels of political consciousness and the manner in which they view their own responsibility in the struggle for national reconstruction. After the evaluation, which yielded very satisfactory results, the 200 comrades began their participation in an intensive course equivalent to the Preparatory Cycle but with some content material that goes beyond what is usually included in this cycle."

This project illustrates the second major concern that the Commission on Education shares with FARP. The central problem is to find valid routes, consistent with the possibilities within the country, for the continuation of learning begun by members of FARP in the literacy phase of their work. In order to be effective, these routes would have to be available to them whether they remained active in the armed forces or, after demobilization, were incorporated into productive activity in agriculture or in industry. This leads naturally to the third preoccupation of FARP, the Party and the government: the whole question of the appropriate reorientation of the former military personnel into other activities.

"The majority of those who are demobilized," said Julio de Carvalho, "will be sent into productive activities in the rural areas since agriculture is our principal activity. However, there are some small and middle-level industrial units—like the refining of sugar, for example—into which a certain number of those who leave the military will be integrated. This month (March 1977) we have begun with the first group to establish a production cooperative as a pilot program. In this whole process we are planning to continue to demonstrate the unity between production and education, work and study. We are intensely interested in readying these former soldiers for activities like the preparation of land for cultivation, as well as other agricultural work, including planting sugar cane, starting fruit orchards and planting rice. We therefore see this production cooperative as an experiment from which we can learn how to develop similar ventures for children and young people. Such experiments will form a natural bridge between schools and production. The Commissions on Agriculture, Health and Education are immensely interested in the experiment and cooperating with us in what we all feel is in accord with the spirit of PAIGC and closely related to the program that the Commission on Education is carrying out on a national scale.

"If we are successful," concluded Julio de Carvalho, "we hope that by the end of the year we will have developed a model that can be useful in other areas of the country with the appropriate changes required in each area.

## Notebooks for Learners

Returning to literacy education for civilian adults, we must mention the initiatives taken in the preparation of materials. Literacy education as cultural action cannot, as I have said so often, use traditional primers. Instead, a notebook has been prepared. At Mario Cabral's suggestion, it has been called *Nô Pintcha—A First Notebook for Popular Education.* It is similar to the one Elza and I suggested for use in Saõ Tomé e Principe except, of course, that it conforms to the realities of life in Guinea-Bissau.

It has two parts, or two "moments," dynamically related to each other. There are three objectives for the *First Notebook for Popular Education:* to offer the learners support and greater security during their learning while at the same time stimulating their creativity; to make possible an easy and rapid transition to

post-literacy; and to assist the leaders in their political-pedagogical task.

We will seek to analyze, one by one, the two "moments" of
the notebook. In the first, the learners begin their experiences
in reading and writing the linguistic symbols associated with the
"reading" and "rereading" of aspects of reality represented in
the codifications. It is the moment that requires serious attention to decoding the meaning of the codification to which the
generative word refers, and to oral expression by the learners
of their critical analysis of the codified situation.

This first part of the notebook contains, therefore, all of
the generative words—in Guinea this means 20 words—associated with the corresponding codifications. From the first
to the ninth word there is nothing except the codification,
the generative word that refers to it and, immediately following this, the word broken down into its syllables. Then there
follow two blank sheets that invite the creativity of the learners, who will write on them the words that they are themselves creating through the combination of syllables. Later
they will be able to compose, little by little, phrases and
sentences—their own texts.

There is a necessary time allowed for the creative experience
of the learners who, in the act of decoding their own reality, get
practice in entering into some of its aspects as well as of analyzing the generative word. They learn how to take the generative
word apart into its syllables and, in the moment of synthesis, to
put it back together as a generative word after they have discovered the other words they can make with it. It is in this sense
that literacy education as a cultural act in a revolutionary perspective is also an act of learning in which the learners are the
active Subjects.

Only between the ninth and tenth generative words does
what I call the "first book" of the learner appear—even
though this expression is not written anywhere in the notebook. It is a simple, direct text made up of words—none of
which is outside the possible combinations that the nine generative words offered. In the final analysis, this simple text is
also a codification written in accessible language. It should

be treated as just this. It is not put into the notebook purely as a reading exercise, nor as a text to be memorized or repeated over and over as is often done in traditional literacy classes. It is intended, rather, as an exercise—the first that these learners will ever have—in critical reading that goes beyond its own superficial structure to reach its deeper structure of meaning, through which the relation between the text and its social context can be understood.

Up to this point, the learners will have had experience in "reading" reality through decoding photos and drawings. Now they will be invited to make this same kind of "reading" of reality through a written text. For this reason it is very important to pay serious attention to the interpretation of the text—which should be "rewritten" orally by the learners.

For the tenth through fourteenth generative words, the same procedure is followed: codification; the generative word that refers to it; the taking apart of the generative word; and the two blank pages.

Encouraged by the creative experience that they have been having ever since the beginning of the activities in the Culture Circle—of creating their own words—and stimulated by the reading of the first text, some of the learners may, at this point, begin to write on the blank pages, not only words, but short texts also. And they should be encouraged to do so.

Between the fourteenth and fifteenth generative words, the second text, a little longer than the first and a bit more difficult, is introduced. It should also become the object of critical analysis and be "rewritten" orally by the learners.

Now that they have mastered 14 words and have had the experience of reading two texts, the learners are ready for a series of creative exercises that must be constantly invented and reinvented in close relation to the reality of the place where the Culture Circle is being held. One example appropriate for the learners in Bissau or in other urban centers would be for the learners to copy in their notebooks some of the slogans of the Party that they see in posters or written on the walls of buildings. They could add to these selections from the newspaper *Nô Pintcha*. This material, collected by the learners and their leader, could be read aloud and then become the object of analysis by all in the Culture Circle.

In this way progress would be made in integrating the "reading" of reality through the decoding of photographs and drawings (or codifications) with the reading of texts related to the context and the integration of both of these "readings" with the practice of writing. It would also be very important, on the other hand, to start with the motivation that the notebook can evoke and to study the possibility of close collaboration between the Coordinating Commission, the newspaper *Nô Pintcha,* and the national radio. This same kind of collaboration is now being studied in Saõ Tomé e Principe.

A page in the newspaper that might serve the learners and their leaders in the Culture Circles could be extremely useful. Such a page could carry news of what is happening in the Circles —the progress and problems of the learners and the solutions that have been found for some of these. It might also contain short articles written by some of the learners as well as summaries of some of the discussions about certain themes of national interest. Such a page would reinforce the support given to the learners by their notebooks: it would offer them more reading material and would also provide material about themselves and a means for them to speak.

As far as the radio goes, there is a whole world of possibilities. There could be programs that broadcast some of the debates taking place in the Culture Circles. Or the Coordinating Commission could analyze the recorded debates and actually create programs that might motivate listeners to organize Culture Circles in their own homes, on their streets, and in their neighborhoods.

Such a program—called, perhaps, "A Culture Circle in Your Home"—could be transmitted initially through a radio broadcast and later transmitted over loudspeakers in different neighborhoods of the city—in Bissau, at least—from the headquarters of the Circles or from the Party offices. Such a program could contribute to the political formation of the population.

Two more texts appear in the first part of the Notebook: between the eighteenth and nineteenth generative words and following the twentieth and last word. Both are from Amilcar Cabral, the second being on the subject of the unity between Guinea and the Cape Verde Islands.*

The second moment of the Notebook situates the learners clearly in the transition phase between literacy and post-literacy education. I shall not speak here of the methodological aspects —the exercises that reinforce learning, those that aid in word recognition, others that help overcome early learning difficulties. These are all exercises that are used as they are needed now that the learners are reading and writing and as they begin to take another step in their search.

In summary, the second part of the *First Notebook for Popular Education* is introduced by a text in two or three sections with the objective of motivation. It contains eight codifications without, obviously, any generative words—since that phase is completed. There follow some blank pages and, then, four texts from Amilcar Cabral about forms of resistance—economic, political, cultural and by force.

The eight codifications are photographs—some of them quite beautiful. All are related to eight national "generative themes": production, defense, education—both formal and nonformal, health, culture and the role of workers (both peasants and urban workers, of women and of youth) in the task of national reconstruction.

Amilcar Cabral's texts are interwoven with the codifications without in any way suggesting that they are the decodification of what appears in the photographs. The decoding task belongs to the learners and the leaders together. They do it orally at first and then in writing. In the transition between literacy education and post-literacy studies, the learners thus continue to deepen their learning and simultaneously to intensify their ability to express themselves in both written and spoken form.

The material that is produced during this phase is immensely rich—revealing not only the learners' capacity for graphic ex-

---

*At the suggestion of Miguel D'Arcy de Oliveira from the IDAC team, four pages near the beginning of the notebook have only the places marked for the codifications and the syllabic families to be derived from any generative word. Whenever one of the Culture Circles wants to add or substitute a codification and its generative word, it can do so by filling in the blank spaces.

pression but also their comprehension of national reality.

Some of these works born in the Culture Circles and written in the *First Notebook for Popular Education* could come to constitute the first volume of a collection of "peoples' texts" much like those that, many years ago, were born among the people of Montevideo and published as *You Live as You Can*—a book filled with beauty and strength. Perhaps it is a book forbidden in the Montevideo of today.

The Notebook was prepared entirely in Bissau under the direction of the Coordinating Commission. When all the texts had been selected and edited and the layout completed, it was submitted to Commissioner Mario Cabral, and to Comrade José Araujo, the Secretary for Organization of the Party who had the responsibility of making the final decision regarding the printing. Claudius Ceccon of the IDAC team had added the final artistic touches—the organization of graphics, the placement of photographs and the type to be used.

All indications are that other notebooks will follow the first as soon as the work advances and the post-literacy phase begins to demand them. The national teams' experience with the use of the first Notebook will prepare them for those that will come later.

## A Visit to the Maxim Gorki Center at Có

This postscript would not be complete without some reference to our latest trip to Có where Elza, Julio de Santa Ana, Regula, a journalist from Switzerland, and I spent three days living with the 60 teachers studying there and the permanent teaching staff.

I was interested during those days of life together to test some of what I had said earlier about the Center. I had the draft of the introduction to this book with me and I read the pages about Có very carefully during my short stay.

It was a great satisfaction to find all of the fundamental things that I had written confirmed by my conversations with the leaders of the program and by our visits to the agricultural fields. The joyous confusion in the mornings at six when everyone takes part in physical exercise; the trips to the settlements around the Center where the Culture Circles continue to function in spite of some linguistic problems not too different from those at Sedengal; the regular seminars that we sat in on, deeply impressed by the life and dynamism of the discussions—all confirmed my earlier enthusiasm for the Center.

Something new and extremely interesting has been started. Another Swiss woman, also by coincidence named Regula, is working with them in an investigation of cultural and historical aspects of the area. Initially they are recording stories and memories of the older people, recording thus the collective memory of the people themselves.*

We participated in a meeting of the whole body—students and teachers—at Có. I read a few pages from the introduction to this book—those that described my experiences at Có. Afterwards, there was a general conversation, the theme of which became increasingly focused on an understanding of the Center as part of that great continuity of educational experience that began and developed in the older liberated zones during the struggle. Then the discussion returned to Amilcar Cabral. I continued to have the impression that they felt him as a presence, very real to them now, and not as a myth from the past. They spoke of his extraordinary vision; of his capacity to foresee what would come about; of his dreams and of his influence.

"Amilcar Cabral has not died. He continues living in us," said one of those present. "All that he spoke of is being born day by day in our work. Many of the dreams that he dreamed—dreams of the people, our dreams—are now being realized. The enemy published throughout the world the news of the death of Cabral, thinking that that would be the end of PAIGC. But PAIGC is not dead. Cabral is not dead. We are all Cabral."

I kept meeting everywhere at Có the same militant spirit. It is present in the most insignificant activities and in the most creative. It can be seen in the cleanliness of the patio of the Center as well as in the enormous care taken, from morning to

---

*One can imagine the importance of a project like this that constantly deepens the roots of the Center in the locality where it is. Even though at the moment, for a number of reasons, it is not possible to go beyond the collection of material through interviews and, I would add, even though there may be some lack of precision in the processing of the interview data, the validity of the project in indisputable.

night, of the banana plantation. It can be seen in the neatness of each private room and in the pounding of the wheat for the bread that all will eat; in the washing of the pots and pans and in the enthusiastic participation of all in the seminars. There is a spirit of unity, of working together as a team in which there is no place for isolationism and privileges, the rights of one against those of others. Social and political responsibility is expressed by those at the Center not only for the Center itself but in the relation of the Center to the people and to the struggle for national reconstruction.

There is no better way to conclude these pages than to quote the words of one of the professors at the Center at Có. His brief comment catches the wonderful spirit of participation, creative discipline and commitment that characterizes the Center. "All of us are responsible *in* the Center and *for* the Center," he said to us, without any other comment.

# FINAL WORD

Without exception, every book that I have written has been a report of some phase of the political-pedagogical activity in which I have been engaged ever since my youth. Some have related experiences already concluded. Others have emerged from the midst of experience as it has been happening. *Pedagogy in Process: The Letters to Guinea-Bissau* is, perhaps, the most explicit of them all, beginning with its title. The introduction and the postscript set the context for the letters. They explain how the letters came to be written.

As the experience described in the book progresses, I will feel obliged to continue to report experiences that may deepen the affirmations and analyses already offered or, indeed, correct some of them. I may add points not treated in this first report on the work in Guinea-Bissau.

One of the points to which I will need to return is that of language. The deeper I go in the Guinean experience, the more importance this problem assumes. It demands different responses under different circumstances. The fact is that language is inevitably one of the major preoccupations of a society which, liberating itself from colonialism and refusing to be drawn into neocolonialism, searches for its own re-creation. In the struggle to re-create a society, the reconquest by the people of their own word becomes a fundamental factor.

# NOTES

## Introduction

1. In this connection see the critique of colonial education in Tanzania by Julius Nyerere in "Education for Self-Reliance," in *Essays on Socialism* (London and New York: Oxford University Press, 1968).

2. See Franz Fanon, *The Wretched of the Earth* (New York: Grove Press, 1965), and Albert Memmi, *The Colonizer and the Colonized* (New York: Beacon Press, 1965).

3. Amilcar Cabral, *Unité et lutte*, vol. 1, *L'arme de la théorie* (Paris: Cahiers Libres–Maspéro, 1975), pp. 302–3.

4. Ibid., pp. 200–201.

5. Fourth Centenary of the Publication of The Lusiads, Commission for Commemoration in Guinea: *Os Lusiadas e a Guiné Bissau* (1972).

6. From a speech of the President of the Council of State, Luiz Cabral, delivered at the opening of the second session of the first People's National Legislative Assembly, April 22, 1976.

7. Amilcar Cabral, "Sur la Petite Bourgeoisie," in *L'arme de la théorie*, pp. 301–3.

8. Ibid., p. 320.

9. Amilcar Cabral, *PAIGC—Unidade e Luta* (Lisbon: Publicações Nova Aurora, 1974), pp. 12–13.

10. In this connection see Harry Braverman, *Labor and Monopoly Capital: The Degradation of Work in the Twentieth Century* (New York and London: Monthly Review Press, 1974).

11. Amilcar Cabral, *PAIGC—Unidade e Luta*, p. 14.

## Letters

1. Amilcar Cabral, *L'arme de la théorie*, p. 303.
2. Ibid., p. 324.
3. Karl Marx, *El Capital (Capital)*, vol. 1, p. 138 (Mexico Fondo de Cultura Económica).
4. Samir Amin, *Eloge du Socialisme* (Paris: Editions Anthropos).
5. Karl Marx, *El Capital*, vol. 1, p. 137.
6. Ibid., p. 130.
7. Julius Nyerere, "Education for Self-Reliance," in *Essays on Socialism*, p. 61.
8. In this connection see the work of Albert Memmi, *The Colonizer and the Colonized.*
9. See Louise Jean Calvert, *Linguistique et Colonialisme: Petit traité de glottophaigie* (Paris: Payot, 1974).
10. Karel Kosik, *Dialética de lo Concreto* (Mexico: Editorial Crijalbo, 1967), p. 25.
11. Ibid., p. 26.
12. H.P. Lee, "Education and Rural Development in China Today," in *World Yearbook of Education*, vol. 5, *Education and Rural Development* (University of London and Institute of Education, Teachers' College, Columbia University, New York, 1974); quoted in *Literacy Work*, vol. 4, no. 2 (October–December 1974), p. 55.
13. *China! Inside the People's Republic*, by the Committee of Concerned Asian Scholars (New York: Bantam Books, 1972), p. 158.
14. With reference to this point see Paul T.K. Lin, "Development Guided by Values: Comments on China's Road and Its Implications," in *On the Creation of a Just World Order*, ed. Saul K. Mendlowitz (New York: The Free Press, 1975), pp. 259–97.
15. Amilcar Cabral, *PAIGC—Unidade e Luta*, p. 46.
16. Ibid., pp. 219–20.
17. Ibid., p. 59.
18. Ibid., pp. 14–15.

## Postscript

1. *Diario de Lisboa*, April 1977.